NEVER SAY DIE

The Story of David Yone Mo
and the Myanmar Young Crusaders

NEVER SAY DIE

The Story of David Yone Mo
and the Myanmar Young Crusaders

Douglas Hsu

ANM
publishers

NEVER SAY DIE

The Story of David Yone Mo
and the Myanmar Young Crusaders

© 2009 by Advancing Native Missions

ISBN: 978-0-9715346-1-2 Paperback

Published by:

ANM
publishers

Advancing Native Missions
P.O. Box 5303
Charlottesville, VA 22905
www.adnamis.org

This book is dedicated to
my beloved wife Indira,
who has faithfully stood by my side for the past ten years
and who has never given up on me.

Many women do noble things,
but you surpass them all.
Proverbs 31:29

CONTENTS

ACKNOWLEDGMENTS

First of all, I would like to thank the Lord Jesus Christ for giving me extra grace to write this book. Without His help, I am absolutely certain that I would not have been able to complete this task.

I would also like to thank my dear wife, Indira, for standing by my side throughout the entire length of this challenging project. It is her unfailing moral support and encouragement which has pushed and prodded me to write and finish this book.

Special thanks goes to Ron Tillett for helping support this project financially and morally, to Joel Maas for assistance in selecting photographs, and to Bill James for layout and printing.

Last but not least, I would like to thank all the staff and friends of Myanmar Young Crusaders whom I had the privilege of interviewing during my research visit in 2002. Your honest and heartfelt testimonies have found their way into the pages of this book.

INTRODUCTION

His father wanted him to become an engineer. His mother wanted him to become a doctor.

But David Yone Mo ended up becoming the leader of Burma's number one street gang.

This book tells the story of one of the greatest human miracles in 20th century Asia: the transformation of Burma's most reckless gangster into one of the country's most outstanding preachers and social workers. After God healed him supernaturally on his deathbed, this ex-heroin addict literally became a father to thousands of drug addicts, orphans, lepers and HIV-AIDS patients across his nation.

The backdrop to David's life story is the fascinating Southeast Asian nation of Myanmar, formerly known as Burma. Politically, Myanmar is known for its isolationist military government with a questionable human rights record. Culturally, it is known for its staggering ethnic diversity: roughly two-thirds of the population are ethnic Burmans, while the rest consists of over 130 officially recognized different tribes. And religiously, it is known for its overwhelming Buddhist majority.

Unfortunately, Myanmar's most famous export in recent years has been heroin. The infamous "Golden Triangle" region comprised of Myanmar, Laos, and Thailand accounted for most of the world's heroin supply up through the 1990s. From this area blanketed with opium poppy fields, the poppies are processed into opium and the opium into heroin. For many years, Myanmar held the dubious honor of being the world's leading exporter of heroin.

Myanmar's heroin has not only ravaged the lives of millions in the West, but it has also ruined countless Burmese lives too. Heroin addiction and its inevitable consequences such as crime and HIV-AIDS continue to be monumental problems for millions of Burmese, especially the youth. In light of these sobering facts, the life and work of the late Rev. Dr. David Yone Mo take on even greater significance.

I wish to mention two quick notes for the reader. First, in light of the present military regime and the Buddhist establishment in Myanmar, I have tried to be as sensitive as possible in avoiding unnecessary criticism of either of these two institutions. The Lord gave David tremendous wisdom in establishing his ministry without antagonizing either of them; and prudence obviously dictates that I do the same, for the sake of the continued well-being of the ministry.

Second, I have chosen to use the names "Burma" and "Rangoon" when referring to events that took place before 1989, the year in which the military government suddenly decided to re-name the country and its main cities according to their original names. For events that took place after this time, I have used the new names "Myanmar" and "Yangon," respectively.

I do hope the Lord ignites a fire in your heart and in your spirit as you read this account, however imperfect it may be, of David's life and ministry. Many times while writing this book, I found myself pausing and asking, "Am I like this, too? Can I be like this, too?" I hope you ask yourself the same questions as you read it for yourself.

Douglas Hsu
New Delhi, India
October 2008

CHAPTER 1
The Young Rebel
(1944-1960)

The principal scowled and looked straight into Elizabeth's eyes. "Your son keeps on getting into fights. These days, it's with boys from higher classes."

Visibly embarrassed, Elizabeth glanced at her teenage son David, who was sitting next to her with his head bowed.

"I'm truly very sorry," she apologized. "Please be assured that I'll handle this matter at home with his father."

"That's what you say every time, Daw Elizabeth," replied the principal, his eyebrows raised, "but I have yet to see any change in his conduct. David is a bright boy, but he's getting into far too much trouble. If this continues to happen, I shall have no choice but to ask you to withdraw your son from the school."

Once they had left the principal's office and exited the school gate, Elizabeth paused on the sidewalk and abruptly wheeled around to face her son, who seemed hardly bothered by the incident.

"I'm sick and tired of your behavior!" she vented. "When are you going to change and stop being a disgrace to your family?"

Unfortunately, Elizabeth knew her son too well to expect a miraculous turnaround. Nothing, it seemed, could get him to stop fighting—neither his father's rod of discipline nor her tearful pleadings. What would it take to bring him to his senses?

From his early days, David had always been restless. Born October 5, 1944, he was initially named Sando, after an Indian hero. Later his mother changed his name to David, after he dreamed as a young boy that he had single-handedly killed a bear and a wolf.

Like his Biblical namesake, young David was strong, tough, and fearless—but in all the wrong ways. Although he excelled in athletics, and especially football, where he was selected as high school team captain, he channeled most of his energy into fighting. From an early age, he began picking fights with other schoolboys—and winning. No amount of punishment, whether from the school or from his parents, seemed to have any effect on him. Winning fights afforded him a short-cut to popularity, and David never seemed to mind paying the price. When no one in his own class dared fight him anymore, he started picking fights with older boys.

David's behavior was all the more surprising, considering that he was born into one of Burma's most distinguished families. His father, Yone Mo, came from a hard-working Chinese immigrant family. Orphaned at a young age, Yone Mo was raised by his elder sisters, who sacrificed to give their brother the best education possible in Burma (then still a part of British India). He earned a national Gold Medal award in chemistry, which netted him a prestigious scholarship to study engineering in London. There he met his future wife, Elizabeth Sein Pu, a Burmese woman who had also received a prestigious scholarship to study nurs-

David's parents, Yone Mo and Elizabeth Sein Pu

ing in London after overcoming fierce odds. Born into a Karen tribal family, she grew up shuttling back and forth between her separated parents. Yet in spite of her family circumstances, she managed to secure the top rank in her nursing class and landed a scholarship to become the first Burmese nurse to graduate from London.

After completing their studies abroad, both Yone Mo and Elizabeth returned to Burma and married. Their stellar academic credentials paved the way for brilliant careers. Yone Mo eventually became the Commissioner of Burma Railways, and Elizabeth served as chief nurse assisting the newly formed Burma National Army (founded by the country's national hero, General Aung San). The couple settled in Rangoon, the nation's capital, and soon became one of the city's well-known elite families. They had five children—three sons and two daughters—and naturally expected each one of them to follow in their bright footsteps.

But while his siblings worked hard in school and brought honor to the family name, David had little patience for books, even though he was gifted with a sharp mind. Happy-go-lucky to a fault, he preferred channeling his energies elsewhere: playing sports (football and weightlifting), flirting with girls, and getting into fights. By his teenage years, he had clearly become the black sheep of the family, and his parents were at a complete loss as to how to handle him. Elizabeth even enrolled him in classical violin lessons, hoping that this would calm her wild son. But David showed little interest in music until a certain musical import reached Burma's shores from the other side of the world—Elvis Presley.

"Elvis-mania" swept the Burmese upper-class youth in the late 1950s, and David was determined not to be left behind. He dropped his violin, picked up a guitar, and taught himself how to play. Soon he was singing Elvis hits to the wild delight of all his school buddies. *"Ain't nothing but a hound dog…" "Love me tender…"* The words rolled off his tongue as smooth as honey.

His golden voice and rebellious temperament were a perfect match for this trendy musical import called rock-and-roll. Immediately David became a sensation among his friends, who frequently gathered around him just to listen. He sang at party after party, endearing himself to many dreamy-eyed girls. He was even asked to sing Elvis over the local radio station!

During his mid-teen years, David's conduct slid from bad to worse. Behind his parents' backs he started smoking cigarettes and marijuana and drinking alcohol. He always had plenty of money to spend, because he always knew how to sweet-talk his mother into giving him ample pocket money. With this amount he would generously purchase cigarettes, marijuana, and beer for his growing circle of delinquent friends. They would frequent the local cinema halls, where they could smoke freely under cover of darkness. On weekends he would go out on the pretext that he was spending the night at a friend's house, when in reality he would be partying outside with his buddies. Everyone loved to party with David, because he usually offered to pick up the bill for their food and drink.

By this point, David's academic performance had fallen off so much that it was doubtful whether he would even pass his matric exam—the grueling national board exam given to all tenth-class students. Even though his parents and teachers knew he was highly intelligent, they were fed up with running after him to make him study.

"David, if you manage to pass your matric exams, then I'll jump off the fourth floor of the school building!" his math teacher scoffed at him one day in frustration.

Never one to back down from a challenge—and particularly one as exciting as this—David applied himself to his studies with rare concentration. The stunning result: not only did he pass, but he passed with academic distinction! He gleefully brought his mark sheet to show his math teacher and watched in sheer delight as she looked it over, dumbfounded. When she had finished reviewing it, he politely responded with a devilish grin, "See, Miss? I fulfilled my end of the challenge. Now it's your turn to fulfill yours!"

For once, his parents were proud of his academic performance. With his surprisingly high marks, David secured admission into Burma's most prestigious institution, Rangoon University, as a science and engineering student. Finally, it seemed, he was living up to the Yone Mo family name.

But the greater freedom from the gaze of his parents and teachers proved to be too much for David to handle. Once he arrived at the university, he completely abandoned his studies and plunged into a life of sin. He successfully turned the men's common room into a gambling den. Instead of attending classes, he would spend his days smoking marijuana, gambling, and drinking. To fund his vices, he would visit local shops and demand "protection money" from them: if they gave him money, he promised to protect them from outside troublemakers. And wherever he went, he would get in fights and beat people up— sometimes to settle a score, and sometimes just for fun.

But all his rebellious behavior to date would seem like child's play once he discovered the street gangs of Rangoon. No one could have predicted how quickly his life would spiral downhill in the days ahead.

CHAPTER 2
The Road Devils
(1960-1963)

David was half-drunk when the other gang leader picked up two machetes to challenge him.

"Who do you think you are, anyway?" snarled the other fellow, also reeking of alcohol. "You take one machete. I'll take the other. Come on, show me what you're made of!"

Unfazed, David whipped out a razor blade from his back pocket and snapped it in half. He gave one piece to his challenger and looked him straight in the eye.

"Forget about machetes. We're using these!" David retorted. And gesturing to a barrel a few feet away, he continued. "Come on, let's jump into that barrel and cut each other to pieces. You show me what you're made of!"

Fearful of the outcome, the other contender backed down, and David further cemented his reputation as the most fearless and reckless gangster on the streets of Rangoon. At 5'9" and 160 pounds (73 kg), he was big for a Burmese and could easily fight four men by himself. It was just a matter of time before he became the undisputed leader of Burma's largest and most notorious street gang: the Road Devils.

Patterned after a British street gang, the Road Devils were Burma's version of America's "Hell's Angels." Sporting shoulder-length black hair, tough-looking beards, and leather jackets with axes, knives, and other weapons tucked into their blue jeans, the Road Devils cruised the town on motorcycles looking for trouble. They drank hard, gambled hard, and fought hard, using switchblades, crowbars, and cycle chains. It didn't take long for David to get drawn into the gang soon after entering the university. Already a boozer and a brawler, he found gang life much more thrilling than simply partying with his own group of friends.

With his fellow gang members at his side, David would often stroll into a bar for a few drinks. After downing a few bottles of alcohol, he would be in the mood for a fight. It didn't take much to set him off: something as trivial as a little beer foam from someone else's mug landing on his shirt was all the provocation he needed.

"Hey! What did you do that for?" David would yell at the other guy, half-drunk.

And in a matter of seconds, the entire bar would be drawn into a senseless fight. When David and his fellow Road Devils had finished thrashing the other fellow and his friends, they would regain their composure, wipe the sweat off their foreheads, and swagger out looking for more trouble.

Under David's leadership, the Road Devils soon took control of the streets of Rangoon. As gang leader, he wasted no time putting his fearless spirit and able mind to work. He visited the U.S. Information Service Library in Rangoon and read books on his heroes— American mafia kingpins such as Al Capone and Lucky Luciano—from whom he learned everything he needed to know about how to run an underworld gang. Aside from making sure that the Road Devils remained unrivalled on the streets, his top priority was ensuring a constant flow of money and alcohol to his fellow gang members.

To accomplish this, David mastered the art of extortion. For example, he would target the various illegal gambling dens across the city. He would select a time when he knew that the den owners and their customers would be present. Then he would take a dozen of his axe-and-chain-wielding gang members with him and suddenly crash their gambling hideout. Terrified at the prospect of being publicly exposed and equally afraid of being beaten up by the Road Devils, the den owners had no choice but to pay David a large sum of money to avoid "trouble."

From time to time, David would re-visit these same gambling dens to collect more extortion payments. He also used these same tactics on the many illegal homemade liquor (moonshine) shops around town to extort free alcohol. In this way, he successfully financed his gang's boozing and brawling.

At the same time, David used the Road Devils to fulfill his own "Robin Hood" quest for social justice. Whenever he had the opportunity to help a poor person, he would take the law into his own hands and do so—especially if it came at the expense of the rich. Sometimes he would seize land from wealthy landowners and distribute it among several poor families. Other times he would use his own money to buy food for a hungry family or pay off a poor man's debt. If he heard that a rich fellow got a girl pregnant and later dumped her, he would hunt him down and teach him a lesson by breaking both of his legs with a bamboo pole.

Through these "Robin Hood" acts of justice, David quickly became a hero in the eyes of Rangoon's poor, who loved him and always shielded him from the police. As a result, the police were never able to nab him. The rich victims of his aggression always remained silent, fearing further trouble from David and his gang. It may have seemed odd for such a notorious gangster to be so concerned about the poor, but God was already at work in David's heart, laying the foundation for the extreme compassion that would one day characterize his ministry.

What was it that drove David to such heights—and depths—of human behavior? He was fueled by a tremendous ambition to reach the top, as his parents had done, but not through the conventional way of education. He knew that he was intelligent, but he didn't want to study. Later in life he would confess, "I wanted to sit on top of those who had degrees, and I had decided that the best way to reach this goal was through lawlessness."

Not surprisingly, David's academic life plummeted. He flunked his first year of university and was forced to repeat the same year at a local college. Somehow he managed to pass and was re-admitted to Rangoon University in 1962 as a second-year student.

But dramatic political events cut short David's university days. The Burmese military staged a coup in March 1962, abruptly changing the country's political course. Massive student demonstrations at Rangoon University broke out a few months later, protesting the establishment of a military dictatorship. In response, the military cracked down on the student dissenters, arresting and killing many of them. David was in the student crowd when the army began firing. He dove into a nearby ditch and escaped unharmed, but many of his classmates and friends were not so fortunate.

With Rangoon University embroiled in political turmoil, David dropped out of school. His father got him a job as an apprentice engineer at a dockyard, hoping that this would provide some desperately needed structure to his son's life. But instead of mending his ways, David simply carried over his gangster habits into his new environment. He regularly offered his co-workers alcohol and managed to get them drunk most of the time. After a few months, David's supervisor was so furious that he transferred him onto a ship to work as a seaman. But there, too, David brought his sins along with him. Drunk much of the time, he quarreled and fought with the other seamen so much that they started plotting ways to push him off the ship into the ocean.

David's parents, desperate to see their son settled, managed to open one last employment door for him at the American Embassy in Rangoon.

"Please, David," his mother warned, "don't do anything to lose this job! You've already disgraced your family enough. If you get yourself into a mess again, I don't think we can do anything more for you."

But his mother's words had little effect on him. He continued drinking heavily, which led to repeated problems on the job. One day while drunk, he got into a fight with another staff member and knocked out three of his teeth. As a result, the American embassy promptly fired him. But David didn't mind, as he was hardly interested in holding down a regular job. Instead, he decided he would simply devote his energies now to pursuing the three things that appealed to him the most: wine, wealth, and women.

Just how successful he would be at pursuing women, he was soon about to discover.

CHAPTER 3
Kathy
(1963-1974)

Blessed with good looks, an athletic build, and a golden voice, David had become a typical Romeo by his mid-teens. He had enjoyed a string of pretty girlfriends since high school, always taking a different one out each time to the cinema or to a dance, and he was always interested in meeting new ones.

One day at a party, he came across two new girls who caught his eye. It turned out they were sisters from the Philippines. The older one was Kathy, a Catholic primary school teacher. The younger one was Caroline, a nightclub singer. Both had pretty faces, like Asian actresses. The main difference between the two was temperament: Caroline was loud, flashy, and flirty, while Kathy was quiet and reserved.

David wanted to get to know both of them better, so he took turns taking them out for spins on his motorcycle. Both of the sisters, like dozens of girls before them, were swept off their feet by the romantic attention heaped upon them by the dashing young hero. But David decided that he liked Kathy better than her younger sister, because of her calm spirit and sense of domestic responsibility. He continued taking her out, and before long the two had fallen in love. They even started talking about marriage.

But when Kathy raised the subject with her parents, they were totally against it. "He's younger than you—by two years!" they protested. "And besides, the boy is unstable. He doesn't even have a job! How will he support you?"

David's parents were similarly opposed to the idea of his marrying an older girl, as it ran counter to traditional Asian norms. But determined to follow their own hearts rather than their parents' counsel, David and Kathy decided to elope—much to the shock, outrage, and bitter disappointment of their families, especially Kathy's. Shortly afterwards, to legalize their union, they held a small wedding on July 27th, 1963. David's aunts organized the ceremony, as both sets of parents had refused to bless their marriage. He was not yet even 19; she was 21.

David and Kathy's wedding, July 27, 1963

Kathy, as it turned out, paid an incredibly high price for marrying David. Some time after the wedding, she brought over a copy of the newspaper to show David.

"Look at this," she pointed, her eyes welling with tears. "I can't believe that I'm reading this…"

Her parents had published a notice in the newspaper stating that they had disowned her, because she had married against their wishes and had thereby brought shame upon the family.

David read the article and put his arm around Kathy. "Don't worry, my love," he quickly assured her, wiping away her tears. "I promise you won't have any regrets over marrying me! I'll make it all up to you. Don't worry!"

But this was much easier said than done. The newlyweds' bliss was short-lived, as Kathy soon discovered the truth about David's gang involvement. He had managed to keep it a secret from her before their wedding, correctly assuming that she wouldn't have married him if she had known he was involved with a gang. The moment she found out, she began pleading with him to quit the Road Devils.

"I don't mind if we're poor, David—we don't need that money! Just please leave the gang! For my sake, please!"

But by then, David had already sunk in his roots too deep to pull himself out. He had become addicted to drinking, gambling, and fighting, and he was trapped in this lifestyle of sin. He found himself always quarreling with Kathy over money, as she would argue with him every time he took their grocery money to buy alcohol or cover his gambling losses.

Things slid from bad to worse. After marriage, David began to secretly experiment with the newest drug on the street—heroin. Smoking it was pleasant, but injecting it intravenously gave him a far better "high." By the time Kathy discovered that he was using drugs, it was too late. He had already become a heroin addict.

To support his increasingly expensive drug habit, David resorted to cruder and cruder forms of extortion and crime. He hired himself out as a professional thug, taking money to beat up others—usually by breaking their legs with a bamboo pole. He visited the docks at night after the sea fishing boats were done unloading the day's catch, in order to extort fish—which he would then turn around and sell the next morning. He opened a secret gambling hall in his family compound, from where he would regularly collect dues. He returned to his alma mater, Rangoon University, and started to supply heroin to the rich students there. Not surprisingly, many of them quickly became drug addicts. He even stole jewelry and other valuables from his parents' home, substituted them with clever fakes, and sold off the originals to purchase drugs.

The burden of David's reckless lifestyle grew increasingly heavier on Kathy. Over a ten-year period, five children—four sons and a daughter—were born to them: Mark (1964), Kevin (1966), Sharon

(1968), David Jr. (1970), and Timothy (1973). The responsibility for raising them was left entirely to Kathy, as David was rarely at home during those years. When he did return home, it was usually late at night, when he was drunk and violent. The children would hide under the bed when they heard their father coming in. He would enter the house ranting and raving, and often he would beat Kathy—sometimes hitting her with his hands, other times kicking her. Once he even tried to strangle her while she was pregnant with their last son, Timothy, but five-year-old Sharon took a broom and struck him from behind. When David whirled around to see who had hit him, Kathy jumped through the window and fled. Sometimes she had no choice but to leave her children and run to her in-laws' home for protection.

David had long since stopped taking financial responsibility for his family, leaving it to his parents to support Kathy and his children while he was out drinking and drugging. Kathy had to hide from David the money she received from his parents, because she knew he would misuse it if it came into his hands. When he was broke and needed more money to buy drugs and alcohol, he would bully Kathy to hand over the family grocery money.

"Give it to me! After all, it came from my mother!" he would demand.

When Kathy resisted, David's temper would flare up dangerously. On one occasion, he even threatened her with a meat knife if she didn't hand over the money to him.

David's mother, broken-hearted at seeing her grandchildren growing up in this unstable environment, decided with Kathy's approval to shift the children to her place. The children only went home during their school holidays. In spite of all this, David did not change his ways, nor did he seem to care.

Kathy was at a complete loss as to how to handle her out-of-control husband. No amount of quarreling, pleading, reasoning, or crying could make him change. In private, she threatened many times to leave him, but she could never bring herself to do it on account of the children. But in public, she remained unswervingly faithful to her husband.

Her own father approached her one day and said, "Kathy, I'm taking our entire family back to the Philippines. Why don't you come with us? Leave behind your good-for-nothing husband and start your life all over again there!"

Kathy was moved by her father's offer, especially because she knew she had brought him shame by rejecting his counsel years ago. With loving respect she answered him, "Thank you, Papa, for your gracious invitation. But I married David because I love him, and I will continue to stay with him. You all go back to the Philippines. I will stay behind with my husband and children."

Only one thing kept Kathy sane throughout all those terrible years: her unshakable faith in Jesus Christ. She had become a born-again Christian a few years earlier through the influence of David's mother, Elizabeth, who used to frequently come and support her in David's absence. Although Elizabeth herself grew up as a nominal Christian, she became born-again later in life through the ministry of a Burmese evangelist. Once her heart was filled with God's true peace and joy, she immediately began sharing her new faith with her children. David, predictably, had no interest in religion. But Kathy hung on to every word her mother-in-law shared. Before long she, too, had decided to commit her life to Jesus Christ. In Him, Kathy found not only the strength to carry on from day to day, but also the only hope for her wayward husband.

Elizabeth and Kathy quickly became close, as their hearts were knit together by a common love for Jesus and a common heartache for David. While he was out brawling and boozing, Elizabeth would regularly come over and pray together with Kathy. Often he would return home drunk or high and find his mother and his wife on their knees, together praying for him.

Upset by this sight, he would lash out, "Who invited you here, Mama? Shut up and get out! Enough of you ladies trying to shove your religion down my throat!"

Undeterred, Elizabeth and Kathy would continue to pray for him regularly. But heaven seemed deaf to their prayers. David's addiction to heroin grew increasingly worse, and along with it, his health. At one point, Kathy even had to go out herself and buy heroin for him, because his withdrawal symptoms were so severe.

After many years of drug use, David's weight dropped to 115 pounds. His strength was gone and his eyes turned a sickly yellow. Something was wrong inside his body, and he knew it. Kathy kept prodding him to see a doctor, but he stubbornly refused to do so.

Finally, in a rare admission of weakness, he agreed to go for a medical check-up. His mother took him to Rangoon General Hospital while Kathy stayed home to watch the children. By this time, David was so weak that he scarcely had the strength to walk into the waiting hall.

The doctor quickly examined David, asked a few questions, and began nodding his head knowingly. It was obvious that he had seen plenty of other patients with the same illness. He scribbled something on a notepad and mumbled something to a nurse, who called in a stretcher and asked David to lie down on it. Without any explanation, he was taken out of the room and wheeled down the corridor.

Meanwhile, a hundred questions raced through David's mind. *What's the matter with me? Is it serious? Will I be all right? Where are they taking me? How long before I recover?*

He was about to find out.

CHAPTER 4
Dying in Ward 21
(1974)

"Doctor, what's wrong with my son?" asked Elizabeth anxiously. From the doctor's sober expression, she knew it could not be good news.

The doctor locked eyes with Elizabeth and took a deep breath. "I'm sorry to have to say this to you, Daw Elizabeth, but your son has only a week left to live."

His words slammed into Elizabeth's heart like a truck. *What was this?* She could not believe what she was hearing.

"Your son is suffering from the advanced stages of hepatitis, which I assume he contracted through using dirty needles. His liver is grossly enlarged."

Elizabeth was speechless. "But… but isn't there anything you can do for him?"

"If you had brought him in earlier, we might have been able to do something," he replied. "As it is, his case is far too advanced now." Seeing tears in her eyes, the doctor respectfully lowered his gaze.

Elizabeth sat motionless for a few moments, her mind too overwhelmed to handle the news. After a pause, she brushed aside her tears. "So doctor… what do I do now?"

The doctor drew a deep breath before answering. "I'm truly sorry, Daw Elizabeth. But I'm afraid there isn't anything you can do at this point."

The doctor stood up to leave. Elizabeth quickly composed herself and made her way down the corridor to Ward 21 of Rangoon General

Hospital. Entering the room, she saw David lying on a bed. Pale and motionless, his jaundiced eyes staring vacantly at the ceiling, he hardly seemed like the rough-and-tough boy she had fret over all these years.

"What did the doctor say?" asked David weakly. "I think I'm going to die. My body feels like I'm going to die."

Elizabeth forced a smile and replied, "You'll be fine. Just rest and follow the doctor's orders."

"Don't try to cover up the truth, Mum," moaned David. "If I die, I die!"

Even on his deathbed, David did not like pretending. He knew what kind of patients were sent to Ward 21: hepatitis cases. A couple of his former drug buddies had breathed their last here. Looking around at the other patients in the room, he realized his condition must be as pathetic as theirs.

"It's hepatitis, isn't it?" David asked, with eyebrows raised. "I heard the doctor say something about my liver, and I know who ends up in Ward 21. So how many days do I have left?"

Caught off guard by her son's straightforward talk, Elizabeth's eyes briefly flashed a combination of dread and alarm. But trying her best not to let David sense her thoughts, she quickly grabbed his limp hand and scolded him. "Enough, enough! The doctor said not to get overly excited, or else you'll get worse. Just rest quietly for some time, and talk later when you have more strength."

The conversation fizzled into an awkward silence. Elizabeth had nothing more to say, so she just closed her eyes and prayed quietly. Meanwhile, David could do nothing but lie on his bed and watch his mother's lips move silently. For a man who had prided himself on leading Burma's toughest street gang, this was the absolute lowest he had ever sunk: lying helplessly in a hospital ward for the dying, watching his mother perform the last rites over his body.

David tried turning over on his side, but a sharp pain ripped through his abdomen and he gave up the effort. *Am I really going to die?* he wondered. He thought about a few friends who had contracted hepatitis from dirty needles and never recovered. How did he ever get this disease in the first place? *I never used dirty needles!* Or did he? When he was in desperate need of a heroin fix, he didn't care where the needles came from. Whose needle had infected him, anyway? *When I get out of this place, I'll search out the **** who poisoned me and teach him a good lesson!*

He looked around the room again. The other patients lying there all looked as dull and sickly as he did. *We're all wondering who's going to die next,* he thought. Occasionally one of them groaned in terrible pain. Every few minutes a nurse would come in to check on a patient, scribble something down, and hurry out as if she was fleeing a cloud of poisonous gas. *So this is what Ward 21 is like.*

Unable to turn on his side, he stared at the ceiling again. *So what if I die? I've lived a full life. I've done everything I wanted to do.* He had won nearly every fight he got into. He had passed his matric exam and made it into Rangoon University. He had tasted nearly every kind of food and drink available, and he could put down as much liquor as anyone he knew. He had dated the prettiest girls of his time. Plus, he had successfully conquered the streets of Burma. He had striven to reach the top, and he had made it there.

"I'll go now, David." His mother's voice startled him out of his thoughts. "I'll go check on Kathy and the children, and I'll come back later."

"Yeah, fine," mumbled David. "Go rest a while—you must be exhausted. Don't worry about me. If I'm not dead by the time you come back, I'll see you later."

"Stop it!" cried Elizabeth, not a bit amused. "There's no point talking like that. Be a good patient. I know you'll be fine—I've been praying to God to heal you."

"Yeah, yeah," he muttered. "I don't think God would even dare touch my cursed body!"

Elizabeth leaned over and tucked something under David's pillow. "I'm putting a Bible here, okay son? It's here just in case you want to read it. If you need some comfort, please turn to—"

"Forget it, Mum!" he interrupted. "I never read it before; do you really think I'll read it now? In this condition?"

Elizabeth squeezed his hand and kissed him lightly on the forehead before leaving. As David watched her go, he thought to himself, *They never quit trying, do they? God knows I don't deserve their love.*

As the hours passed, David drifted in and out of periods of disturbed sleep. His pain was increasing, his strength was failing, and he could feel his mind wandering more. *Is this what it feels like to die?* he wondered. With nothing else to do besides stare at the ceiling, his mind flitted randomly from one subject to another. *What am I really doing on earth, anyway?* Of course, now that he was about to die, he felt bad that he hadn't been a better husband and father. *"I'll do a better job next time,* he thought. But would there be a next time? He had never given much thought to the after-life. *What really happens after death?*

"Give me your arm," said the nurse, jolting him out of his daydream. She had come to check his blood pressure.

"Tell me frankly: am I going to die?" he asked.

The nurse frowned at him. "Don't talk like that. Just take rest and you'll get better," she replied mechanically, before leaving the room.

They're all afraid to tell me the truth, David thought. *What's there to be afraid of death, anyway? Haven't I faced worse enemies in my life? If they only knew who I was, they would know that I'm not afraid of anything!*

But where would he end up, really, after his death? The question nagged at him during his waking hours, even though he tried to tell himself it was foolish to worry about such things. Would he slip into an eternal sleep? Or was there really life beyond death? Was there a God after all? He had never cared about religion growing up, due to his parents' different faiths. His father was a Buddhist; his mother, a Christian. He didn't want to side with either, so he had turned his back on religion at a young age. Back then, God and death and nirvana and heaven had all seemed so impractical and irrelevant, as he was young, tough, and invincible. But now, with death lurking just around the corner, he wished he had the answers to these questions that he had never thought about earlier.

For the first time in his life, he felt uncomfortably alone. While the nurses shuffled in and out of the room and the overhead ceiling fans droned on and on, David tried to close his eyes and sleep, but he could not. *Where did I come from? What am I doing in this world? Where will I go when I die?* The questions kept haunting him, refusing to go away. Even when he tried thinking about other things, it was of no use. His soul was restless, and nothing could give him peace. *But where do I go for answers now?*

Suddenly he remembered the Bible that his mother had tucked under his pillow. *Is it still there?* He reached for it with his right hand. *Yes, it was still there.* He pulled it out. *Would it contain the answers I'm searching for?* Probably, although he had no idea where to look. *So many pages in this book—where the **** do I even begin?* He decided to flip it open randomly, and it fell open at the 23rd chapter of Luke's Gospel. He started reading from there.

David had no idea that the words on that page were about to change his life.

CHAPTER 5
The Canceled Funeral
(1974)

D avid couldn't remember if he had ever picked up a Bible before. But as he started to read the 23rd chapter of Luke's Gospel, he found himself captivated by the story.

> *Two other men, both criminals, were also led out with him to be executed. When they came to the place called the Skull, there they crucified him, along with the criminals— one on his right, the other on his left. Jesus said, "Father, forgive them, for they do not know what they are doing." And they divided up his clothes by casting lots.*
>
> *The people stood watching, and the rulers even sneered at him. They said, "He saved others; let him save himself if he is the Christ of God, the Chosen One..."*
>
> *One of the criminals who hung there hurled insults at him: "Aren't you the Christ? Save yourself and us!"*
>
> *But the other criminal rebuked him. "Don't you fear God," he said, "since you are under the same sentence? We are punished justly, for we are getting what our deeds deserve. But this man has done nothing wrong."*
>
> *Then he said, "Jesus, remember me when you come into your kingdom."*
>
> *Jesus answered him, "I tell you the truth, today you will be with me in paradise."*
>
> Luke 23:32-43 (NIV)

When he had finished reading the story, David paused to reflect. *You are that criminal*, a voice inside him whispered. *You have lived a life displeasing to man and to God. You are that criminal.*

David shuddered. *Was it true?* His mind quickly flashed back over the years—the drinking, the fighting, the gambling, the drugging, the extorting, the wife-beating… *You are that criminal, and you are getting what your deeds deserve*, the inner voice continued, accusingly.

It was true. He couldn't argue with the facts. He had lived a life of lawlessness and had managed to escape punishment most of the time, but his deeds had finally caught up with him. Sure, in his own eyes he was a hero, but in the eyes of the law—and in the eyes of God—he was a criminal. A low-down, vulgar, drug-addicted criminal.

Suddenly David felt naked, as if all his ugliness lay exposed before heaven and earth. He had never felt this way before, as he had always taken pride in his exploits and boasted in his recklessness. But now, after reading this short Bible story, his positive self-image was suddenly shattered. He could finally recognize who he was on the inside, and he didn't like what he was seeing at all.

I've really lived a life displeasing to man and to God, he realized. *My deeds have caught up with me, and I'm getting what I deserve.*

He didn't like feeling this way. Lying alone on a hospital bed, with his life coming to a pathetic end, David was suddenly riddled with guilt and self-disgust. Deep down, he knew what his final destiny would be. And for the first time in his life, he was genuinely afraid.

Is there any way out? He decided to read the same Bible story again. When he came across Jesus' words, *"Today you will be with me in paradise,"* a sudden ray of hope sprang up in him. But David was confused. *Did Jesus really mean that? How could a criminal end up in paradise?* It didn't make any sense for a criminal, who deserved punishment, to be guaranteed a free ticket to paradise.

David scanned the text for answers. The only thing he could find was that the criminal turned to Jesus a few moments before his death, requesting, *"Jesus, remember me when you come into your kingdom."* That was all. Nothing else. *Is that all I have to do, too?*

Suddenly he remembered what his mother always used to say to him: "All you have to do is to believe." Ever since she had become a born-again Christian, she had been running after him to believe in Jesus. But every time she brought up the subject, he would shut her up, saying, "Don't try to shove your religion down my throat!" He didn't need a nagging mother to tell him what to believe.

After his marriage, his mother used to regularly come over to pray for him and Kathy. He would always leave the room, but Kathy would listen carefully to everything she said. Just one year into their marriage, Kathy decided to put her faith in Jesus Christ and was baptized. "Oh great, now I've got not one but two preachers running after me in the family!" he used to complain. David recalled all the times he returned home late at night to find Kathy and his mother together on their knees, praying for him. It made him sick to see them like that.

As he sank deeper and deeper into drugs and crime, Kathy would repeatedly urge him, "It's high time you believe in Jesus Christ and change your ways!" He would always shoot back, "Stop jamming your religion down my throat! I didn't take it from my mother, and I'm not going to take it from you either!"

Back in those days, though, he felt he could conquer the world. But now, with death just a few days away, he knew he desperately needed help. *All you have to do is to believe.* The words rang clear as a bell in his heart. *Believe that Jesus died on the cross to save you from what you deserve: hell.* It all rushed back to him now, his mother's mini-sermons and Kathy's tearful pleadings. But would God really forgive him and accept him?

If Jesus could guarantee a spot in paradise for that criminal, then he can also save me. David knew he didn't have a lot of time left to make things right with God. He prayed softly, *Jesus, I'm sorry. I've made a terrible mess of my life. Please forgive me. Please remember me when you come into your kingdom.*

Right at that moment on August 5, 1974, David felt a tremendous peace flood his heart and a strange, supernatural power surge through his body. He knew instantly that Jesus Christ had answered his prayer! Immediately he jumped off his bed and exclaimed, "Praise the Lord!" The other patients in the room looked at him oddly, as if he were mentally ill.

"Praise the Lord!" he announced to them excitedly. "Jesus Christ just saved me!"

One of the nurses in the corridor saw him walking around the room and was surprised. How did the bedridden patient suddenly get up and start walking? Immediately she rushed into the room and asked him to lie down.

"No, I feel fine!" explained David, ignoring her request.

The nurse went out to call her supervisor, who came in and also asked David to return to his bed.

"Really, I do feel fine!" he insisted. "Actually, I feel great! Let me walk around a bit."

The nurse supervisor turned to the other nurse and whispered, "I think he's in his final death throes. Sometimes they do this just before dying. We need to get him down, though, or the doctor will scold us!"

But David refused to lie down, insisting that he felt much better— to the amazement of the hospital staff. Within a day, his eyes had changed from jaundiced yellow back to white, and his liver pain was gone. When the doctor came in to check on him, he was dumbfounded at David's inexplicable recovery.

"It's all because of Jesus Christ!" David explained excitedly. "Jesus saved me, and he also healed me!"

Unable to offer any other explanation for this sudden turnaround, the doctor could only smile awkwardly.

When Elizabeth and Kathy came to visit him, they were shocked to see David on his feet, walking. But they were even more stunned to hear what he had to say. "Mum! Kathy! I finally surrendered myself to

Jesus Christ! He saved me, and He healed me too! You know how all these years you both teamed up against me, trying to get me to believe in Jesus? Well, two against one—I finally lost!"

At first, Elizabeth and Kathy did not know how to respond. Was David's conversion for real, or was he simply deceiving them again? Several times in the past, he had pretended to become a Christian just to get money out of his mother. After winning her confidence and sweet-talking his way into her purse, he would conveniently leave the faith. This time, to be sure, Kathy and Elizabeth were genuinely impressed by his confession and even more amazed by his dramatic physical improvement. But they remained skeptical: it just seemed too good to be true.

Over the next week, David's health steadily improved day by day. After a few days, the doctor reported to Elizabeth and Kathy that David's hepatitis was "mysteriously" gone, with no medical explanation. The ladies trembled with excitement: *Can this really have happened to David? Lord, it's too good to be true!*

Within a week, David was discharged from the hospital, his recovery having been deemed a medical miracle. Elizabeth brought her son home, where he saw a wooden coffin lying in the corner. Suddenly alarmed at the thought that one of his brothers must have died while he was in the hospital, David blurted out, "Whose coffin is that?"

Elizabeth answered with tears in her eyes, "It's yours! The doctor told me that you had less than a week to live, so I had already made all your funeral arrangements. But I certainly don't mind canceling them!"

Looking at his own coffin, and then at his mother and Kathy, David replied, "The Lord has done something wonderful, and I need to tell others about it!" He hadn't felt this good in years. *My buddies won't believe what happened to me,* he thought. *I need to go find them and at least tell them I'm alive!*

Little could anyone have predicted the effect that the news of David's conversion would have on the streets of Rangoon.

CHAPTER 6
A New Gang: the Myanmar Young Crusaders
(1974-1976)

"Hey, what are you doing here?" exclaimed an astonished Road Devil gang member to David, who had suddenly pulled up on his motorcycle. "We thought we'd never see you again!"

"What did you think—you could get rid of me that easily?" David shot back.

"How did you recover so quickly?" asked another. "We heard you were on your way out—for good!"

"You're not going to believe this, guys," David announced, "but I got HEALED. Totally, completely, miraculously healed. By Jesus Christ!"

"WHAT?"

David proceeded to share his hospital experience with them, while they stared at him in wide-eyed disbelief.

"So Jesus forgave me of all my past sins," concluded David, "and He also healed me on my deathbed! No more sickness, no more alcohol, no more drugs, and no more messed-up living! You guys need to believe in Him, too!"

One by one, the Road Devils shuffled off awkwardly. Some even laughed at him. They had never seen this side of David before, and amongst themselves they dismissed his experience as a temporary "religious high" that would quickly fade away. "He just got out of the hospital, that's why he's talking this way," they said to each other. "Just wait and see—he'll be back to using drugs in a few days."

But contrary to their expectations, David did not go back to drugs, nor did his religious fervor diminish at all. In fact, it only grew more intense as the weeks passed. He refused to give up "preaching" to his gang members, urging them to quit alcohol and drugs in exchange for a new life with Jesus. Even when they approached him for money to drink or gamble with, as was their habit, he would first give them a "sermon" before handing over any money to them. His persistence paid off: several Road Devils were convinced by his message and decided to quit their old ways to follow Jesus. David was thrilled!

"Let's go out together and share this message with others who need to hear it!" David urged them. "Remember, we used to roam the streets to party? How about now roaming the streets to preach?"

So along with his former gang buddies who had decided to follow Jesus, David began actively sharing his conversion experience with anyone who would listen: gang members, friends, beggars, alcoholics and drug addicts. Everyone listened to him, mainly out of curiosity; it was unheard of in those days for a notorious gangster to suddenly "find" religion and have his life transformed overnight. And to David's joy, a growing number of listeners—especially drug addicts—identified closely with his message and responded by saying that they, too, wanted to start following Jesus.

As more and more people starting believing in Jesus through David's testimony, he faced a new challenge: where should he take them to get baptized? He knew that all new believers were supposed to be baptized. But he wasn't qualified to perform baptisms himself, because he wasn't a pastor. Initially he told the new believers to join any local church, where they could receive baptism and be nurtured in their new faith. But the newly-saved drug addicts kept coming back to David with the same problem: no church would invite them in, let alone baptize them!

David could not understand this. *Why would the churches exclude drug addicts?* he wondered. Assuming that there must be some miscommunication and confident that he could resolve it, David approached a local Rangoon church to ask whether they could baptize 16 drug addicts who had recently accepted the Lord. To his amazement, the church refused him. He went to another church, only to receive the same response. After visiting numerous churches and getting the same answer, he finally went to the pastor who had baptized Kathy and requested him to perform the baptisms. As a gesture of goodwill to Kathy, the pastor agreed—but only on the condition that this would be the first and last batch of drug addicts he would ever baptize!

The churches in Burma at that time had never heard of drug addicts or gang members repenting of their sins and getting saved. To them, these "sinners-turned-saints" were simply going through a temporary religious phase before eventually returning to their former ways. Not only did they doubt the genuineness of David's conversion, but they also assumed that his so-called "new believers" were nothing but a group of shady characters following their drug addict leader.

David was disappointed, hurt, and angered by this rejection from the local Rangoon churches. The very community which he had counted on to welcome and support him was, in fact, the same one pushing him away. *They have no idea what God is doing, nor are they open to hearing about it,* he realized. But David had no time to wallow in self-pity or bitterness. The bottom of society's barrel—addicts, gang members, and alcoholics—kept on coming to Jesus Christ, and he desperately needed to find a place where they could be baptized and cared for.

To create a new home for his rejected converts as well as to organize his growing evangelistic activities, David decided to start a new Christian gang in place of the Road Devils, which had disbanded in the absence of his leadership. He named it the *Myanmar Young Crusaders*, or MYC for short. Approximately 50 MYC new believers began meeting for worship on Saturday evenings in his own family compound, under the shade of a large tamarind tree. David himself served as the "pastor" of this growing congregation of addicts as well as non-addicts.

David also came up with a new slogan for his ministry: *Never Say Die*. It appealed greatly to drug addicts and alcoholics, because it reminded them that one never has to die if one has Jesus Christ. It was also intriguing to Buddhists, who did not believe in eternal life and were therefore curious to learn more about its meaning. David began using this slogan everywhere he went.

News of David's incredible transformation continued to spread throughout Rangoon. Gone was his gangster look: long hair, leather jacket, and blue jeans. He had cut his hair and started wearing traditional Burmese dress— a Burmese jacket with a *lungi* (skirt-like cloth wrap)—in order to gain the respect of a wider audience. Gone too was his gangster behavior: smoking, drinking, drugging, gambling, swearing, and fighting. Few who had known him earlier could recognize him now, so different was his appearance and behavior after his conversion.

Perhaps the most striking change about David was his fervent zeal to tell anyone and everyone about Jesus Christ. Along with his band of new Christian disciples—mostly ex-gang members and ex-addicts—he began taking his message to the streets of Rangoon: in the marketplaces, on the buses, and even aboard docked ships. The public was intrigued by his message and his approach, for this kind of street evangelism had not been seen in Burma for many generations.

"I've got good news to tell you, and you need to listen!" David would announce through a megaphone during a typical street outreach, interrupting the normal hustle-bustle of a Rangoon bazaar. Out of curiosity, the local people would pause from their marketing and gather around.

"I've got some little booklets that I want to give each one of you—for free!" he would proclaim, grabbing their interest. "But first, please give me a few minutes of your time so I can tell you something about *life*."

With the mostly Buddhist crowd listening intently, he would continue his message using simple illustrations. "If you came here and managed to get a free bag of rice, you would be very happy, wouldn't you? But how long would your happiness last? One day? Two days? Only as long as the bag of rice would last, right? So wouldn't you like to know how to be happy for a lifetime?"

He would go on to share about Jesus Christ and the eternal happiness available to those who believe in him. Knowing that his Buddhist listeners had no guarantee of their own salvation, he would boldly proclaim, "We cannot achieve salvation by our own merit. But Jesus Christ can save you! Would you like to try him out for yourself?"

When he was done speaking, David and his MYC disciples would distribute free gospel tracts to the crowd. Through these street outreaches, many in Rangoon heard the gospel message for the first time, and more new believers were added to the MYC fellowship under the tamarind tree.

God honored the simple, bold faith of David and his band of zealous followers by protecting them from police harassment. Whenever David staged an outdoor preaching event, the police would naturally assume that it must be an impromptu political rally, which was forbidden by the military government. Time and time again the police would question David, "Who gave you permission to do this?" And time and time again, David would simply brush them off, as he used to do in the past while he was a gangster.

On one occasion, while David was preaching in the open marketplace, several policemen with guns approached and asked to speak with him.

"Not until I finish my preaching!" replied David brashly.

"You're very bold to say that to us," the policemen responded. "Who do you think you are?"

"I've come here to tell good news to the people," David explained. "But if you'd like to, go ahead and shoot me!"

Unaccustomed to such boldness, but also uncertain as to whether David was actually breaking the law, the policemen waited until he was done speaking before commanding him and his teammates to report to the police station. Upon reaching there, the policemen asked him, "Where did you get permission to speak like this? You need a permit for this kind of function."

David answered, "The director of our board gave us the permit."

"Who is the director? Where is the permit?" asked the police.

"If the director comes himself, then does he need to bring the permit?" questioned David.

"If the permit was issued by him, then no," came the answer.

"Well, I am the director!" replied David, smiling triumphantly.

The policemen were suddenly embarrassed: they had unknowingly harassed the director of the board! Apologizing profusely to David, they insisted that he and his teammates stay for tea and cakes before leaving. David and his comrades laughed all the way home: the Lord had been good to them!

While a great deal of David's energy was focused on his growing ministry, he also knew that he had to properly take care of Kathy and their five young children—something he had totally neglected to do all these years. After his conversion, he realized what a terrible, irresponsible husband and father he had been, and he was determined to make things right.

As the weeks and months went by, David gradually won back the confidence of his children. Kathy, too, began to trust that the changes in her husband's life were genuine, and for the first time in their eleven years of marriage she started to feel hopeful inside.

But what could he do to earn an honest living? Up till then, he had only known how to make money through crooked means.

"Don't worry," Kathy consoled him. "I've managed to save a little money, which should last us for a few months." Having been forced to run the household on a meager budget for many years due to David's addictions, Kathy was used to lean times.

"But that money won't last forever," David countered. "How about I use that money to start a pig business? If we pray beforehand, I know the Lord will surely bless it!"

Kathy had her doubts, but in the end she decided to trust her faith-filled husband. The couple prayed: *Lord, we want you to be a partner of our business: 50-50. Fifty percent of the profit we'll keep, and fifty percent we'll give to you.*

David took the money which Kathy had saved—1,000 kyats—and went out to purchase a pig. He returned home, rejoicing. "I got this one for an excellent price!" he beamed.

Kathy was not impressed, however. The sow was ugly, with an upturned nose. Her disapproval quickly turned to anger when she learned that David had been cheated: the seller had knowingly given him an infertile pig! "I told you, what do you know about pigs?" she wailed. "Now we've even lost our meager savings!"

"Have faith in God," David tried to assure her. Privately, he started to pray even harder: *Lord, please get me out of this mess! I got stuck with an infertile pig!*

A male pig passed by one day, and David's sow got pregnant—miraculously. He prayed again: *Lord, let her give birth to a super-size litter!* (A normal litter was six or seven piglets.) It seemed like God was answering David's prayers, because his pig grew unusually large, almost like a hippo. She consumed so much food that David had to borrow money from ten people just to pay for its feed.

As the time for delivery drew near, David slept over the pigpen just to make sure that no piglets would be lost during the birth. And sure enough, God honored David's prayer: his "infertile" sow delivered a whopping 15 piglets!

David sold ten piglets to pay off his creditors and kept the remaining five. The Lord's hand was upon his business, and eventually he had 70 pigs. After some time, however, he told Kathy, "I don't think the Lord gave me a new lease on life just to run a piggery!"

So after praying about this matter, they agreed to sell the business in order to concentrate full-time on the ministry. *Lord, last time we offered you 50% of the profits, and you blessed us so much. This time, we'll give you 100% of the profits—just give us a good buyer!*

Some time later, one of David's friends shared that he had just received a grant from the United Nations to start a government piggery. Would David be willing to sell his super-fertile pigs to him? Immediately David knew this was the Lord's answer to their prayers! With the proceeds from the pig sale, he built a 40-foot by 80-foot brick fellowship hall in his family compound, adjacent to his house. (He had previously constructed the foundation with the 15,000 kyats that his mother had given him as an advance share of his inheritance.) Thanks to his mother and a herd of blessed pigs, the MYC believers no longer had to crowd under a tamarind tree to worship the Lord.

With a proper fellowship hall constructed, David was finally able to accommodate the physical growth of his ministry in his own family compound. However, he was feeling increasingly inadequate to handle growth in the other aspects: street evangelism, instructing new believers (especially drug addicts), and running a church. After all, he had no previous church or ministry experience to guide him, nor did he have anyone to help him. *If only I could get some training, I could help these people better*, he thought.

In 1976 he learned of a training opportunity with Campus Crusade for Christ, which involved spending two months learning evangelism on the Coco Islands (located off the southern coast of Burma). He jumped at the offer, sensing this was a once-in-a-lifetime opportunity.

David had no idea that this brief trip would forever alter the course of his ministry, as well as the musical landscape of Burma.

CHAPTER 7
The Seven Lean Years (I)
(1976-1979)

The warm sea breeze felt good on David's face. He was sitting outside on a large rock in the Coco Islands, reading his Bible during a break from evangelism training. The soothing rhythm of the ocean waves relaxed his spirit, and before long he drifted off to sleep.

While asleep, David had a strange yet wonderful dream. He was singing and playing guitar with a large rock band—singing Christian songs set to pop/rock music. Thousands of people were listening in the crowd, while David and his fellow musicians performed into the night.

He awoke from the vision, confused. What was the meaning of it? In those days, Christian music in Burma consisted of traditional hymns. There was no such thing as modern or contemporary Christian music. What did guitars and rock concerts have to do with Jesus? It all seemed impractical and irrelevant, so David just dismissed it and went back to reading his Bible.

After completing his two-month evangelism training, David sailed back to Rangoon. At the arrival dock, three young men whom he had never met before were waiting to meet him.

"Uncle, we're Christian musicians," they introduced themselves. "We play guitar and drums. We want to record a gospel album set to pop music, but we need two things: a good vocalist and someone to help us finance the project. We heard that you used to be an excellent singer, so we've been eagerly waiting for you to come back and join our team. Will you?"

David was taken aback by their invitation. Did this have anything to do with his Coco Island vision?

"Well, I used to sing, but that was a long time ago," he answered hesitatingly. "I don't know anything about gospel pop music—I've never even heard of it. Plus, it takes a lot of money to put together an album, you know. That's one thing I don't have a lot of."

But drawn to their enthusiasm and also sensing that this was the Lord's will, David agreed to work with them. Aside from being musically talented, these young men were risk-takers, and David liked that.

First, they had to raise enough money to buy an amplifier and finance the album project. The group members pooled their resources together and sold a few personal items. But still they needed a lot more money.

Always the adventurous, risk-taking sort, David then returned home, pulled out all his extra clothes, and sold them. After that, he went into the kitchen and started taking down cooking pots from the shelves.

"What are you doing?" asked Kathy curiously.

"We need some more money for the album project," he explained a bit sheepishly. "We're not using these pots anyway, are we?" he asked.

"No, go ahead and sell them," replied Kathy with a gentle smile, careful not to dampen her husband's enthusiasm. For years she had been used to seeing her husband sell their household belongings to buy drugs. Now that he was selling the same things to serve the Lord, all she could do was to quietly thank God in her heart. What a miraculous transformation!

After a while, David came back in the house and started picking up pieces of furniture. "I need to sell these, too," he explained to Kathy, "but I promise to buy new ones once we get some more money."

"Go ahead," she replied supportively.

"And these dining chairs—" he said, lifting them up, "do you mind if I take these, too?"

"No, that's fine," she answered. "We can always spread mats on the floor to eat."

But the money was still short. What could he do? He had already sold everything in the house that he could think of. Only one thing was left: his wedding ring. Seeing no other option, he decided to quietly sell it, too. Kathy later noticed it missing from his hand and asked him about it.

"I sold it for the album money," he replied. "Anyway, the gold ring won't last, but what we do for the Lord will last!"

At these words, Kathy immediately removed her wedding ring—her only piece of gold left—and put it in David's hand. "Then please take this, too, and use it for the Lord," she said to his astonishment.

Though David certainly felt guilty selling off his family possessions one by one for what seemed like a crazy venture, deep down he had a peace from the Lord that he was doing the right thing. It was a thrill to lay everything on the altar for Jesus, and all the more so because he knew that Kathy was standing right beside him.

The album was released in 1976 as a MYC label, under the title *God Loves You and Died for You.* The lyrics were solidly Christian, and the music was guitar-and-drums country jazz featuring David as one of the lead singers. For its time, the album was revolutionary: nothing like it had ever been produced by Burma's Christian community. (In those days, drums were still considered taboo by the church establishment.)

The MYC album became an overnight hit. News of its release spread like wildfire among the churches. Area Christian leaders touted the new album as further proof that MYC was a Christian cult: "Road Devils, drug addicts, and now drums!" But the more they attacked the "cult music," the more their young people wanted to listen to it! For Burma's Christian youth, guitars and drums represented a refreshing change from the traditional piano-and-organ-led hymns.

"Jesus likes organs, but I don't think he has anything against drums," replied David wryly to his critics. "Besides, if the Lord isn't in our ministry, I'm sure He will shut us down soon enough!"

MYC conducting a musical outreach meeting in a rented facility, late 1970s

But the Lord didn't shut MYC down. On the contrary, his ministry exploded with growth. After David started incorporating this new country jazz gospel music in his ministry, over 300 people began attending his Sunday worship services—a six-fold jump over the 50 who used to huddle under the tamarind tree. On Saturdays, he would conduct a "sing-song" service featuring guitars and drums. For these services, he purchased a small cheap amplifier, which used to cut out intermittently. Someone would have to hit it every so often just to keep it working. On Wednesdays he led a prayer meeting. David served as pastor, Bible teacher, drug rehab counselor and band member. Although he was often tired, he couldn't have been happier.

Encouraged by the spectacular response to MYC's album, David began incorporating this new gospel pop music in his city-wide evangelistic outreaches. *"Min gala ba!"* (Greetings!) he would announce through a megaphone. "God bless you all! We'd like to present you a song about God's love for mankind and God's love for you."

In the open markets, at train stations, on school campuses and aboard steamers, the crowds would stand still and listen attentively to the well-dressed young men and women singing catchy gospel tunes, accompanied by guitars and tambourines. The music would be followed by a brief message, in which David would often share one of his favorite verses, 2 Corinthians 5:17—*"Therefore if any man be in Christ, he is a new creature: old things are passed away; behold, all things are become new."*(KJV)

Afterwards, the MYC team members would distribute free gospel tracts with the address of the MYC compound, 108 Insein Road. On a regular basis, interested seekers ranging from drug addicts to Buddhist monks would visit the MYC campus after reading the tracts, and a good number of them eventually became followers of Christ.

By this time, a growing number of drug addicts and alcoholics had already accepted the Lord through David's ministry. For various reasons, most of them ended up staying long-term with David at the MYC compound. For one, they often had nowhere else to go: many had been chased out by their own families after repeatedly stealing to buy drugs. For another, they knew that if they left MYC, they would probably end up right back where they started. Furthermore, they truly felt the love of God there, especially as they knew that no other church or ministry would have anything to do with them.

So within a couple of years' time, about 20 male ex-addicts had joined the MYC community as residents. At night, they would roll out their bedding mats and sleep on the floor of the fellowship hall. In the morning, they would roll up their mats, leaving the space free for classes and meetings.

David had no training in drug rehabilitation, so he had to rely solely upon the Lord to guide him. In the early years, there was no structured rehab program or well-developed system of rules and regulations. The MYC compound functioned more or less like a Christian commune for ex-addicts and ex-alcoholics, and the residents had a considerable amount of freedom. To the best of his ability, David would prepare Bible lessons for them, to help them stay off drugs and alcohol and grow in their new faith. Not surprisingly, over half of these new believers backslid and returned to their former ways.

David wasn't the only one who stayed busy during these years. Kathy took it upon herself to cook every day for the growing MYC community, even though she often didn't know where the provisions for the next meal would come from. Sometimes the rice would be finished, and she would quietly inform David that there was nothing left to cook. He, in turn, would announce to the young men: "Today we're going to have a day of fasting and prayer!"

Yet somehow, the Lord never failed to provide for the MYC family. For example, during one "fasting and prayer" day, an unfamiliar jeep suddenly pulled into the MYC compound. A lady doctor stepped down from the vehicle and instructed her driver to open the rear door. To David's amazement, there were several large sacks of rice, dried fish, and potatoes inside! The doctor explained that the Lord had strangely laid it upon her heart earlier that same day to buy this food and deliver it here. As the young men carried the sacks of food into the kitchen storeroom, they realized that it was completely empty. God had provided just in time—again!

Family photo, circa 1978-79. Front row, left to right: Timothy, David, Kathy.
Back row: Sharon, Kevin, Mark, David Jr.

Through such incidents, the Lord greatly strengthened the faith of the growing MYC community during the "seven lean years" (1974-1981). David and Kathy went through great financial difficulties during this period. Sometimes they had no idea where the next day's provisions would come from. Occasionally they had to sell their own personal items in order to make ends meet. For a man with a wife and five young children to care for, in addition to a growing gang of ex-addicts and ex-alcoholics for whom he had assumed full responsibility, these were indeed challenging years. David's mother helped out as much as she could; but with nearly 30 mouths to feed, her assistance could only go so far. However, as David witnessed the Lord's miraculous provision time and time again, he realized that Jesus Christ was no ordinary god. He was the Living God, the God Who Sees, Jehovah Jireh. And through each trial and test, the Lord was forging David's character and building up his faith.

Even though his plate was more than full at home, David began sensing that the Lord was calling him to take his message beyond Rangoon. *The Lord is doing an amazing work in our midst, and it's not fair to keep it to ourselves!* he thought. He became burdened for the hundreds of thousands of drug addicts across the country who needed to hear that Jesus Christ could set them free. He knew that God had given him a testimony and a message. And he knew that God had also uniquely blessed him with a strategic musical bridge to reach them.

So David began taking his MYC gospel team by bus and by train to different Burmese states to conduct "mini-crusades." He would select a rural area surrounded by lots of country villages, knowing that in such places there were sure to be many addicts and alcoholics. (In rural Burma, especially in the hill regions blanketed with opium poppy fields, teenagers and adults often had nothing better to do than to drink country liquor and/or use drugs.) The mere fact that a group of outsiders had showed up with guitars and drums was enough to send several hundred farmers scurrying out to watch David and his team play guitars, sing songs, and preach the gospel. At the end of each meeting, David would give an altar call; and nearly every time, people would come forward to accept Jesus as Savior.

How could David afford to take the MYC gospel team out on the road, when he was already facing such great financial pressures at home? Sometimes love offerings from the churches which hosted them would cover their travel expenses. On other occasions, David and his team had to come up with their own travel money by selling their *lungis* (cloth wraps) or furniture. In such circumstances, the MYC gospel team would have to walk long distances and share their clothing with each other, but they didn't mind. They were simply filled with joy at the thought of being like the early disciples: serving the Lord with reckless abandon.

As David's ministry grew, so did the number of his critics. Initially, all the mainline churches rejected him and refused to extend fellowship to his group of believers. Most of the leading ministers felt that David and his other ex-addict believers were "faking" their Christianity: how could drug addicts ever hope to truly change? Every drug addict they had ever known who had turned to "religion" eventually backslid and returned to their old ways.

Several ministers went so far as to circulate newsletters stating that MYC was a misguided cult. How could a genuine preacher talk about Road Devils and Jesus Christ in the same breath? How could somebody who had never graduated from university—let alone Bible school—pretend to teach others about spiritual issues, and particularly when he himself was a former drug addict and gangster? Others objected to MYC's street evangelism campaigns, arguing that preaching should be done in church buildings and not in public places. Still others scorned the community living aspect of MYC, predicting that the entire ministry would soon degenerate into a den of debauchery.

But David was far too busy caring for his new flock to worry about what others thought. "Let them think what they want. I know Jesus is with us!" he would remind his followers. He trusted that it would be just a matter of time before the Christian establishment would recognize God's seal of blessing upon his ministry and repent of its judgmental attitudes.

In fact, during these early years, David received much more harassment from fellow Christians than he did from non-Christians. But the Lord Himself made sure that no outside pressure—whether from the Christian churches, the military government, or the Buddhist establishment—would be able to shut down MYC. At the outset of his ministry, the government's intelligence agency—undoubtedly having heard reports of a new religious movement in the capital city—sent an informer to spy on David and his work. In the course of attending the gospel meetings, the informer became personally convicted of his own sin and decided to accept the Lord. (He later became a pastor under MYC.)

In 1979, while in the midst of these ministry trials, David suddenly got a visa to visit the United States. Some of his siblings had already settled down over there, and he had never visited them. His mother offered to purchase his flight ticket, removing a major obstacle for him to go. "Your sister will be applying for a U.S. green card for you," Elizabeth shared with her son, "just in case you decide to settle down there with your family." She had been increasingly concerned about David's ability to provide for his family, knowing that her grandchildren sometimes had scarcely enough to eat.

David's heart raced. *Lord, maybe this is a new door you're opening up for me and my family!* he thought excitedly. *Please show me Your will in this!*

He was about to find out.

CHAPTER 8
The Seven Lean Years (II)
(1979-1981)

*A*merica *is indeed a wonderful place to be,* David thought to himself soon after reaching its shores. *No wonder nearly every Burmese dreams of going to America, with its promise of freedom, opportunity, and prosperity.* Although he was no stranger to riches, having grown up in an affluent family, David was still impressed with the standard of living in the U.S. In addition, he was overwhelmed by the sheer number of gospel-minded churches and ministries that seemed to be on every corner. In Burma, he was considered an odd religious rebel. But here, he was just one among tens of thousands of born-again Christian ministry workers.

The weeks flew by, and before long he had received his U.S. green card, courtesy of his siblings. Clutching it in his hands, he closed his eyes and thanked the Lord. *Now I can bring Kathy and the kids over here and finally give them the future they deserve,* he thought. *No more lean years for our family and ministry! I'll work hard and send lots of money back home to help the new believers and ex-addicts.*

But the longer he stayed in America, the more restless he became. He soon realized that God was testing him, just as He had tested Moses: would he remain in the comfortable palace with the king, or would he choose to suffer with his own people in the wilderness? As he kept thinking about the perishing souls in his homeland, he realized that God was not asking him to give more money to Burma. God was asking him to give something far greater: his own life.

Lord, I came to this country to seek the good life, David confessed, *but thank you for stopping me in my tracks. I'll return home and do those ministries that nobody else wants to do—even if others call me crazy.* So after six months, David surrendered his U.S. green card to the shock of his relatives and flew back home.

But David's U.S. visit was not fruitless. Before he left, he paid a visit to Liberty University in Lynchburg, Virginia, where he was given many excellent Bible study and correspondence course materials to take back with him to translate. The Bible study materials proved to be immensely helpful, providing MYC with its first structured approach to systematic Bible teaching. The correspondence course materials also proved to be a huge blessing, as MYC could now start offering free Bible correspondence courses to any interested seekers.

David also visited Christian Aid Mission in Charlottesville, Virginia. There he met the mission's overseas director, Carl Gordon, whose friendship would last a lifetime and would prove extremely valuable in the years ahead. Impressed by David's testimony and ministry, Christian Aid began sending US $100 per month to MYC—the first help from outside Burma and further confirmation to David that God's hand of blessing was upon his ministry.

After returning from the U.S., David led a long-distance MYC gospel trip to Myitkyina, capital of Kachin State in northern Burma. What made this trip particularly unusual was that on his way back to Rangoon, David brought along 19 Kachin drug addicts with him! Sixteen of those backslid, but three remained faithful to the Lord.

One of the three was Zaw Naw, a young addict who had attended one of David's crusades. His father approached David at the end of the crusade and invited him to stay in his home. His son Zaw Naw was desperately trying to quit drugs, he explained, but could not. Would David be willing to take him to Rangoon and help him there?

David told the young man, "If you're willing to completely give up heroin from this moment on, I'll take you home with me. But if you use again while I'm here, then forget it!"

Early the next morning, while it was still half-dark, David stepped outside to relieve himself. Suddenly he heard footsteps: it was Zaw Naw, who had come out to get a heroin fix while everyone was still sleeping—or so he thought. David watched quietly as the young man removed a syringe hidden in a tree and jabbed himself in the arm. He remained motionless until he saw Zaw Naw's eyes close shut: the high had come.

Then David suddenly stepped out from the shadows and confronted him. "What's wrong with you, fellow? Your eyes are closed shut!"

Caught in the act, Zaw Naw fumbled for an answer. "You see, sir, we Kachins have squinted eyes, so that's why my eyes appear to be closed shut," he stammered, all the while struggling to keep his eyes propped open with his fingers!

Zaw Naw later apologized and begged David to give him one more chance. Always full of mercy, David agreed. Zaw Naw joined 18 other addicts on the long cross-country trek back to Rangoon, where he became part of the MYC community. Not only did Zaw Naw accept the Lord there, but he later married, had four children, and eventually became the director of MYC's drug rehabilitation program.

Zaw Naw baptizing a new Akha village believer in the jungle, late 1990s

With the sudden influx of nearly 20 new people, the total number of residential ex-addicts jumped from 20 to 40. As a result, MYC's already tight resources were stretched even thinner. Kathy would take several young men with her every morning to the marketplace to beg for free vegetables—usually watercress (the cheapest vegetable) or semi-rotten cabbage. Most days she would make a pot of watery vegetable soup to serve over rice, with a little salt added for flavor. Meat was a luxury, eaten only once a week, and beef tendons at that (the cheapest cut). Occasionally, some well-wishers or relatives of the addicts would bring over a few provisions to help out.

Sometimes the rice would be finished, and there would be no money left to buy more. Without informing anyone of the situation, David would then call for a day of fasting and prayer. Sometimes the Lord would miraculously send an angel of mercy to MYC that day, who was specifically led by God to bring food. At other times, David would suddenly decide to put up a banner outside the MYC gate advertising a Christian movie show that evening. Using a small rented TV, he would charge two or three kyats per person for admission. After taking out the money for the TV rental, he would then use the remaining profit to buy food that evening. Amazingly, Kathy's kitchen fire never went out a single day in all those years—to the glory of God!

The influx of so many new drug addicts also called for significant adjustments on the part of David's family. Due to lack of space, the children often had to stay together with the addicts and alcoholics. Sometimes the addicts, while suffering from withdrawal effects, would lose control over their bowels and pass stool all over the house. Other times they would steal the family's personal items—amplifier, clock, guitar, toys, and once even David's own jacket—in order to sell them for liquor money. On one occasion, David's sons had to chase down an addict who was speeding down the road in a cycle-rickshaw loaded with their own small cycles to sell. And in the most unpleasant incident of all, a drunk resident slapped Kathy in the face while she was serving him food, accusing her of giving him too small a portion.

Incidents such as these caused David to wonder if he was unfairly punishing his family by extending his arms so wide to help others. Was he truly crazy, as many charged? Should he quit? *My kids hardly get to eat meat. If all these addicts weren't around, my kids would be able to eat decently. Plus, they have to deal with guys who pass stool all over their house and sell their toys. As for my wife, she goes out every day begging for groceries, spends the whole day laboring in a hot kitchen, and then gets slapped on the face by a drunkard for whom she cooked and served! Have I gone too far?*

During these times, David understood that Satan was putting these thoughts in his head, so he would reply back to Satan, *So what?* He would remind himself and his family that he, too, used to behave in the exact same terrible manner before the Lord delivered him.

"They're addicts, and they're just behaving like addicts," he would repeatedly assure his family. "Once the drugs get out of them and Jesus gets in, they'll change. If Jesus could change me, I know He can change them too!"

When he had finished consoling his family, he would silently pray, *Lord, you know it isn't easy doing this. But I'll keep my promise to you, to take up those ministries that nobody else wants to do.*

By this time, David and Kathy had already started to relate to the addicts as their own children. All the residents called David "Papa" and Kathy "Mama." Even though the MYC family struggled from day to day, David felt he could no longer think only for his biological children; he also had to think for the needs of his ex-addict children. As the head of a large and growing family, David was always aware of the enormous responsibility he had taken upon his shoulders. Sometimes he felt overwhelmed. *Lord, I know I'm supposed to provide for my family,* he would pray. *But I can't do it alone! You've got to help me!*

Ministering to drug addicts was no easy job, to be sure. Without any professional training, he had to rely on lessons learned from past mistakes and a good deal of prayer to shape his approach to drug rehabilitation. During those early years before he had developed a structured,

Bible-based rehab program, he only took in addicts who had already accepted the Lord. He knew that without Jesus, there was little hope for an addict to change. Even so, over fifty percent of the MYC residents backslid and returned to their former ways. He kept on experimenting with different rehab approaches until he stumbled upon one that seemed to work well: Bible study, Bible study, and more Bible study!

David and the other ex-addict staff leaders whom he had trained started to lead Bible classes twice a day for the addicts: once in the morning and once in the evening. In the afternoons, the residents would do chores while David and his staff team would feverishly prepare for the next lesson. Without any formal Bible training themselves, the leaders had to spend most of their free time studying the Bible themselves in order to teach the next lesson!

David also required the residents to memorize Bible verses, believing that the Spirit of God would always work through the Word of God to transform lives. "No verse, no food!" warned David. "Plus, I'll shave your head!"

These were no empty threats. After going hungry once or twice, the addicts would invariably memorize their verses without fail. Moreover, having a shaved head was culturally shameful in Burma, and those who were disciplined in this manner would have to wear caps during the Sunday services to avoid being humiliated in front of the girls. Even so, David would yank off their caps at an opportune time, eliciting a chorus of giggles from the amused girls!

Besides attending Bible classes and memorizing verses, the residents were expected to attend regular prayer meetings and participate in outreach events. David knew from personal experience how much his own commitment to the Lord had been strengthened through street evangelism. And indeed, testifying publicly to God's work in their lives did help the ex-addicts grow stronger in their faith.

Experience also taught David what rules and regulations were necessary to keep MYC's house in order. In the beginning, residents used to slip out at night and return early in the morning. Some used to smuggle cigarettes into the campus and climb up high in the giant tamarind tree to smoke without being detected. In response, David cut down the trees and established the following basic rules: (1) no drugs, (2) no alcohol, (3) no cigarettes, (4) no medicine without staff knowledge, (5) no violence and (6) no sex.

The first time they broke a rule, they got their heads shaved. The second time, they were asked to leave. But David always leaned on the side of mercy and would give additional chances to offenders whom he sensed were truly repentant.

MYC's new approach began to work, to the surprise of those who never thought a "cold turkey" approach (that is, immediately halting all drug, alcohol, and tobacco use) could ever succeed. As the Lord helped MYC fine-tune its Bible lessons and no-nonsense regulations, its success rate started to climb and outsiders gradually began to take notice.

After seven years of struggle, sweat and sacrifice in the face of widespread criticism, David was ready for a breakthrough in his ministry. Not that he felt like quitting—the word "quit" was not part of his vocabulary—but he did feel in his spirit the need for some divine encouragement.

I'll take up those ministries that no one else will do, he reminded the Lord. *But along the way, please don't forget to give me a boost once in a while!*

David's prayer would soon be answered in an unusual way.

CHAPTER 9
Starting to Reap
(Early to mid-1980s)

"Guess what, Papa?" exclaimed one of the residents to David, who was assisting with the new MYC album sales. "We're all sold out! We need to get more copies—fast—because people are really hungry for it!"

Ever since MYC released its first hit album, *God Loves You and Died for You* (1976), David decided he would produce a new gospel music album every year. Over the next four years, MYC released four new albums, but none of them sold well compared to the first one. The words and the music were too similar to the first album, so there was little demand for them. Confronted with mounting losses, David began wondering whether it was wise to keep on pumping so much time and money into producing new albums.

But everything changed in 1981 with the release of MYC's sixth album, *Everything is Vanity under the Sun*. The young generation simply couldn't get enough of it: copies sold everywhere like hotcakes. The album featured brand new country jazz music and cutting-edge lyrics, both radically innovative for their time. The theme of the album, which ran through all the songs, was that nothing in the world could compare to the love of Jesus. Even the album cover was "cool," featuring a man in a valley of bones. To David's surprise, the album sold well even in the secular market, in spite of its strong religious message.

Within a month of this new release, MYC earned enough from album sales to cover the costs incurred on all six albums combined. Profits kept rolling in, and out of this surplus MYC was finally able to upgrade its musical equipment: better guitars, drums, mixers and amplifiers. This badly-needed upgrade would allow MYC to take its music ministry to the next higher level. Unbelievably, there was still money left over, so David decided to keep it aside to fund future album projects.

Thank you, Lord! Oh, thank you, thank you! David often prayed in those days. For he knew that this amazing success after many years of sacrifice and struggle was nothing less than God's divine blessing.

The soaring popularity of MYC's music naturally led to increased recognition throughout Rangoon. More and more young people from mainline churches started to pour into the MYC church in order to hear this new gospel music. In the process, many accepted Jesus Christ as Savior. And in turn, many of these went back to become ambassadors for Christ—and ambassadors for MYC—in their own homes and churches.

Benjamin's family was a typical example. His two church-going daughters got hooked on MYC's music and decided to attend the MYC service in order to hear the same songs performed live. When Benjamin learned about this, he was furious.

"If either of you ever go back to that cult meeting led by that drug addict," he threatened, "I'll pull you out of school!"

But his two daughters kept on attending the MYC services, because they had found something there that they hadn't found anywhere else: the power of the gospel to change lives. Benjamin became curious as to why his daughters were so drawn to this group. He decided to visit one of the services to see for himself, and in the process he ended up accepting the Lord. (Benjamin later became MYC's accountant.)

The more that young people were drawn to MYC's music-filled church services, the more they accepted Jesus Christ as Lord and Savior. And the more they accepted Jesus Christ, the more their parents and other relatives did also. In fact, soon two-thirds of MYC's new believers were from regular (non-addict) backgrounds. The addition of these new people to the MYC community helped to boost its credibility in the eyes of the public.

But even as the Lord was adding more people in this way, David remained most concerned for the primary group that God had called him to reach: the drug addicts. As word of MYC's success in drug rehabilitation continued to spread, more and more addicts started coming in for treatment. In particular, whenever word got out on the streets that the police were about to do a sweep and arrest all the drunkards and addicts, as many as three men a day would come to MYC and beg for admission.

David hated to turn away any addict, because he knew that apart from Jesus Christ, there was little hope of anyone ever being delivered from drugs and alcohol. The other rehab centers in the country were government-run and had dismally low success rates. But at the same time, he knew that MYC was already operating far above maximum capacity. He could not simply keep on taking in new addicts unless he sent away some of the current ones.

The problem was, no ex-addict ever wanted to leave MYC! For each one of them, MYC had become their new family. David had become their Papa, Kathy had become their Mama, and the other residents had become their brothers who shared a deep bond of mutual understanding. Each one of them had experienced more love, more understanding and more forgiveness at MYC than at anywhere else. How could they leave? And where would they go? Most had no desire to return to their former dead-end home environments. Rather, they wanted to remain indefinitely at MYC and be part of the ministry there.

Another problem was that David had long since run out of teaching material for the residents, as he had completed in just six months' time the entire Bible correspondence course curriculum which he had brought from the U.S. The residents were hungry for more spiritual food, but David didn't have anything else to feed them. A second trip to the U.S. in 1981 enabled David to bring back more Christian books from Liberty University. Upon his return he translated them, and with the help of Christian Aid Mission he was able to print them. But still that was not enough.

Oh, what shall I do, Lord? David prayed. *My hands are full. My house is full. How do I keep feeding these guys—physically and spiritually? Show me your way, Lord!"*

God answered David's prayers in an unexpected way. One day he was approached by a pastor from Chin State, in northwest Burma. The pastor was affiliated with the Evangelical Baptist Conference, a Burmese Baptist group headquartered in Chin State.

"Pastor David, I've heard about you through your music and your gospel crusade teams," said the pastor. "Your testimony is truly inspiring, and I know the changes in your life are genuine. Why don't you pay a visit to our Chin Hills and preach the gospel there? I know your message will bring revival across our state. I'll be more than happy to make arrangements with the different churches in our denomination to receive you. Plus, we'll cover all your travel expenses. What do you say?"

It was an offer too exciting to pass up. David spent three months touring the Chin Hills, sharing his testimony and the gospel in village after village. The ministry was wonderful, but the food was terrible. Particularly offensive to David were the rotten-smelling fermented beans that seemed to appear on his plate at every meal. Out of love for the local people, he forced himself to swallow them, which endeared him even more to his hosts. He was learning a ministry principle which would serve him well throughout the rest of his life: to win the hearts of the people, eat what is set before you, no matter how disgusting it may look or smell!

God blessed David's tour in several ways. One blessing of course was that many people responded to his messages by re-dedicating their lives to the Lord. Another blessing was that David established a lifelong partnership with his denominational host, the Evangelical Baptist Conference (EBC). The EBC was so impressed with David that they appointed him as Vice-Chairman for life. As a result, the hitherto independent MYC church in Rangoon—as well as all future churches established by MYC—would now be affiliated with the EBC. This denominational affiliation would give the MYC churches needed credibility, accountability, and structure.

Perhaps the biggest immediate blessing for David, though, was the "discovery" of Faith Baptist Bible College, an EBC institution in Tiddim, Chin State. The four-year college would be very eager to receive a select number of students from David's ministry, in contrast to other Burmese Christian institutions which would never consider taking in ex-addicts. So David started sending a few of his most promising residents there, after they had completed their six-month course at MYC and had demonstrated sincere zeal to serve the Lord. In four years' time they would emerge well-grounded in God's Word, and they would be much better equipped to help David run the ministry.

"Now what about the other believers, Lord?" asked David. "I need to find a way to feed them too!"

It was true. David's ministry was growing faster than he was able to handle it, or at least it seemed so. Now that the Lord had marvelously opened a door for the ex-addict residents to receive further training, his attention turned to the rest of his sheep. There were the regular Sunday service attendees, who needed more than just a weekly sermon to become well-grounded in the Bible. And there were hundreds—perhaps thousands—of people who had heard the gospel and received the Lord through MYC's city-wide outreaches, but who were never given adequate follow-up counseling or teaching. How could he properly minister to them all? For he did not want to leave behind a trail of spiritual orphans.

As a result, David decided to organize a ten-day leadership training program in mid-April, scheduled to coincide with Burma's national water festival holiday. This would be a ten-day spiritual life camp for anyone who needed to grow in the Lord, primarily directed at outsiders (non-residents). In particular, David was targeting women believers, church members, and new converts from his evangelistic campaigns.

In hindsight, this was an extremely ambitious undertaking for someone who had never formally studied the Bible. A hundred and fifty people showed up, all hungry for spiritual feeding. As soon as the program got under way, David realized that he and his staff needed to study around the clock just to prepare for the next lesson! He could only afford to sleep four or five hours a night, with the rest of his time devoted to studying.

"Turn off the light and sleep!" Kathy would scold her husband. "You'll go crazy!"

But the Lord gave David and his team much grace, and the leadership training program was a huge success. Many became born-again during the program. As a result, David decided that he would make this an annual MYC event.

Meanwhile, as David struggled to keep up with the ministry's expansion, Kathy continued to quietly provide unfailing support on the home front. Aside from shouldering the primary load for raising their five children, she also took full responsibility for feeding the entire MYC residential community, which had grown to nearly 50 people. While her duties, day in and day out and often without adequate funds, would have driven most women insane, Kathy never seemed to complain or grow weary. Everyone at MYC could always count on Mama to be there for them, with her gentle smile.

In 1980 a pastor-evangelist from the Chin Hills came down to Rangoon to attend a ministry conference. He had a young teenage Chin boy with him, who seemed zealous for the Lord. As the pastor was staying in the MYC compound, Kathy asked him about the boy, who was about the same age as her eldest son.

"Ma Na Ling is an orphan," explained the pastor, "His parents died when he was just four years old, so he was sent to live with his uncle, who was the Buddhist high priest in the village. After a few years, his uncle thought it would be good for the boy to also become a Buddhist priest. So after he had completed class four, he was sent to a Buddhist monastery for three years."

The pastor continued, "After three years, the boy returned to his village. There he heard the gospel from an evangelist. The Lord convicted his heart, and he decided to become a Christian. His whole countenance changed after that. It didn't work out for him to stay with his Buddhist relatives anymore, so he ended up at my place, as I am the local pastor. Now he is studying in class eight."

The pastor paused for a moment. "Frankly speaking, even though he's a good boy, I'm finding it hard to keep him with me, because I have four children of my own. I was hoping to find someone or some charity here who could take him in. He's a good boy, really. Plus he has a sincere hunger to know the Lord. Do you have any suggestions?"

Kathy's heart was touched. Even though her hands were already full, she felt that this was a special opportunity that God was giving her. Later she mentioned this to David.

"But the boy is already half-grown!" protested David. "Why do you want to take him in? Don't you think we already have enough people to take care of?"

"One extra person won't matter!" quipped Kathy with a smile. "Besides, an extra child is easier to handle around here than an extra addict!"

So David and Kathy took in their first orphan in 1980. They decided to rename the young teenager Peter, hoping that one day he would live up to his Biblical namesake. They soon discovered that he was an alcoholic, so their first priority was to counsel and pray with him. (It turned out that everyone in his village, including the children, drank homemade rice liquor.) Once Peter fully surrendered himself to the Lord, he was set free from his addiction. From that point on, he began to grow spiritually by leaps and bounds.

(After finishing high school, Peter Ling went on to complete his B.A. from Rangoon University. Meanwhile, he became a powerful evangelist, having learned from Papa how to share the gospel. Recognizing his gifts, David first appointed him as a pastor-evangelist with

MYC, and later as MYC's Bible training director. Eventually David sent him to India to pursue a four-year Masters of Theology course. When he had finished his degree and returned back to Burma, David appointed him to be the principal of MYC's Bible college.)

But Kathy did not stop with Peter. After one year, Peter asked Mama if he could bring his younger brother—about ten years old then—to join him in the Yone Mo family. Kathy agreed, so Ma Na Kee came in 1981. Like his elder brother, he also was an alcoholic, but God set him free after he arrived at David and Kathy's home. And like his elder brother, he also grew up to become a dedicated servant of God. (David later appointed him as secretary over all MYC churches across the country.)

Some time later, Kathy was approached by a woman carrying a day-old infant in her arms. She had heard about MYC's reputation as a charity, and she asked if she could leave her baby with Kathy in exchange for travel fare back to Mandalay. Shocked and disgusted that a mother would be willing to sell her baby for a pittance, Kathy gave her several hundred kyats and took in the infant.

Not long afterwards, a man came to the MYC compound with a two-year-old boy. He was always quarreling with his wife, and they both wanted to divorce each other and start afresh. Their four children—ages five, three, two and one—were "extra baggage," so he was trying to sell them off one by one.

"We'll pay nothing for the child, but you can leave him here if you want," David and Kathy told him.

"How about a bicycle? Will you give me a bicycle for him?" the man asked.

"Absolutely not!" David answered. "Just leave your child and go!"

"In fact," Kathy added, "bring all your four kids here if you want. Whatever you decide, please don't separate the brothers and sisters!" For she understood how important the bonds between siblings were, especially in the absence of parents.

The man took the little boy and went away. Later he returned with three children—the same boy whom he had brought earlier, plus his three-year-old brother and five-year-old sister.

"Where is the youngest child? The baby?" asked Kathy.

"I found someone who would give me a bicycle for him," the man replied.

His eyes glowing with rage, David shouted, "You shameless creature! You and your wife shall never step foot in this place again! Go!"

When David had calmed down, he turned to Kathy and said, "Now we've got three more mouths to feed, plus clothe and send to school! I know you pity every Tom, Dick and Harry, and that's not a bad thing. But how can we take care of them all?"

"The Lord will provide," Kathy assured her husband with a calm smile. "He has in the past, and I know He'll continue to do so in the future."

Kathy was right. As MYC passed through the "seven lean years" and continued to grow and mature, local doubts about David and his ministry began to fade. People gradually realized that his preaching was genuine and biblical, and they could no longer deny the fact that many addicts had dramatically turned their lives around. Area churches that had previously condemned his ministry as an evil cult now began to applaud and support his efforts.

With this shift in attitude towards MYC came additional blessings. Local believers started to contribute whatever they could to the ministry, bringing in small donations of money, rice, cooking oil, and vegetables. One well-wisher donated a potato every day. Others brought in used clothing for the addicts who arrived at MYC's doorstep with nothing but the clothes on their back. A few volunteers started coming in to assist Kathy with her huge cooking responsibilities. Miraculously, even as the MYC residential community expanded, God continued to provide for all their needs.

David rejoiced in all these developments, knowing that after many years of struggle and toil, God was finally vindicating him in the sight of all who had previously dismissed him as a "drug addict Road Devil in preacher's clothing."

"We've been sowing for so many years, and finally—because of God's goodness—we're starting to reap a little!" he said to Kathy. The ex-addicts who were now studying in Bible college, the unexpected popularity of MYC's music, the orphans who had accepted the Lord and who were now studying well, and the gradual recognition among Burma's Christian community that God's hand was upon this "crazy" ministry—these were all fruits that David cherished.

But David had no time to sit back and relax. There was far too much more to be done for the Lord. With renewed energy, he set his face to taking MYC to the next level of radical evangelism and discipleship. All he needed now were a few good men—faithful, reliable and strong men—to help him accomplish his God-given vision.

The Lord was about to surprise him, with His pick of David's future ministry leaders.

CHAPTER 10
David's Mighty Men
(Late 1970s-1980s)

Just before the start of a Saturday evening "sing-song" service in 1979, a fat man sporting long hair stumbled into the MYC campus. He was clearly drunk, as all could see from his talk and his walk. Even so, the greeters warmly welcomed him and showed him to a seat.

The fat Karen man was Albert Howard, an old drinking buddy of David's and a former gangster himself. Even though he had left the gang life after getting married, he still drank heavily. His Christian mother had tried everything to get him to quit, but to no avail. Desperate to see him sober, she had heard about David's dramatic turnaround and thought that perhaps he could help her son.

"There's a church called MYC led by a man who used to be a big-time alcoholic and gangster," his mother told Howard one day. "You probably know him—David Yone Mo. His life totally changed after he dedicated himself to God. He stopped drinking and even became a preacher! Why don't you visit his place? Maybe he can inspire you to stop, too!"

Accustomed to his mother's nagging, Howard dismissed her suggestion. Church was the last place he would ever consider visiting, because he knew from experience that churches were always hostile to alcoholics. Usually the ushers would shoo away people like him at the gate itself, so the holy atmosphere inside would not be contaminated. On a couple of occasions before, Howard had actually made it past the ushers and sat down in a pew. But because his body had reeked of alcohol each time, the church members had held their noses, moved away from him, and given him dirty looks. Furious, Howard had stood up and walked out. After several negative experiences like this, he decided that he would never set foot in a church again.

But Howard began to reconsider his mother's suggestion after one of his drinking buddies began attending the MYC service. "You really ought to visit that church with me," his friend kept saying to him. "It's not like other churches; they actually make people like us feel welcome! Plus, they have great music—not the boring kind that you hear in other places."

Howard was skeptical. But his friend was so persistent that he finally agreed to accompany him one time.

"But let's first drink and then go!" Howard said to his friend.

His breath reeking of alcohol and his teeth stained red from betel nut, Howard stumbled into the MYC campus with his friend one Saturday evening in 1979. He was so drunk that he swayed from side to side. Fully expecting to be turned away at the gate, Howard was surprised when he received a warm welcome and was politely escorted to a seat. No one held their noses, and no one gave him dirty looks. Strangely, everyone seemed friendly and warm. Was it for real?

He was surprised to see his old drinking buddy, David, looking completely different. There was a glow in his face. David came over and greeted him with a huge grin.

"I'm glad to see you here, Howard!" he said. "It's about time you paid us a visit!"

Even though he was drunk, Howard could sense something he had never felt before: the love of Christ. His friend was correct: there *was* something different about this place. Howard really liked the guitar and drums music: it was lively and uplifting. And for the first time, his heart was touched by the message. David spoke about Jesus Christ coming into the world to save sinners, including alcoholics, drug addicts, gamblers and gangsters. *That's me!* thought Howard, as he listened carefully. When the service was over, different church members approached him, thanked him for visiting, and invited him to return the following week.

Drawn by the loving spirit in this place, Howard started faithfully attending services every week. Within a few months, he had decided to accept Jesus Christ as his Savior.

After this, his life changed dramatically. He quit drinking, to the great joy of his family. A gifted singer, he joined the MYC worship team and began serving as a soloist during church services. He started taking leave from his office to join David on MYC gospel outreach trips, where he would volunteer in any way he could: hauling equipment, setting up for outdoor meetings and singing on the worship team. He even began leading a home Bible study group, through which his wife also became a born-again Christian.

Howard's life had never been so full of joy or meaning. In 1981, just two years after his life was touched by Jesus, he resigned from his job with the irrigation department in order to work full-time with David at MYC. Before he made this decision, David had counseled him to prayerfully count the cost. The ministry was struggling financially, as MYC was still in the "seven lean years" period, and there was no guarantee that David could give him a regular salary. But Howard was not deterred. Having seen God honor David's reckless faith and obedience, he was determined to follow in his leader's footsteps.

Howard was one of the earliest of a dozen or so disciples whom the Lord gradually brought into David's life, to help him shoulder the load of his ministry. In the early days, the entire weight of the ministry fell upon David alone: preaching, counseling, administering and disciplining. As the Lord honored David's faithfulness and expanded his ministry, He also began calling other men to help him carry the load—similar to King David's "mighty men" in the Bible (I Chronicles 11:10-11).

These mighty men did not come from stable Christian backgrounds, nor did they have previous ministry experience or Bible school degrees. Rather, just like Jesus' twelve disciples, they were "sinners" whose lives were dramatically transformed after coming into contact with their leader. Most were like Howard and Zaw Naw, former alcoholics or drug addicts who had come to MYC, became born-again, received deliverance from their addictions, and later sensed God calling them to serve alongside David. Some were orphans, like Peter Ling and his younger brother Ma Na Kee, who were adopted by David and Kathy and later caught the MYC vision as they grew older. Each one had a powerful testimony of how Jesus Christ had completely turned his life around through MYC. And each one, because of his outstanding zeal, commitment and courage, eventually became part of MYC's inner circle of leaders.

Howard wasn't the only former drinking buddy of David's to become one of his mighty men. Peter Bo, a Burmese Buddhist, was a classmate friend of David's from primary school. In high school they used to smoke, drink and party together. Both were admitted into Rangoon University at the same time, where they together plunged into a life of gambling, drinking, and smoking marijuana.

Their paths drifted apart after David entered the gang world and got married. Unlike David, Peter managed to complete his university studies and graduated with a degree in English. Later he got married and became a lecturer. But like David, he could not give up his drinking habit after marriage. In fact, he continued to drink daily, which led to increasing problems in his family and on the job. Eventually he lost his job because of his drinking. At that point, he decided to hunt down his old buddy for help.

In 1975, Peter visited David after a gap of many years. He shared his predicament and asked him for some money to drink and gamble with. He was confident that David, who had always been generous with him in the past, would help him out again this time.

"I'll give you the money," answered David, "but first I want you to listen carefully to what I'm going to say."

David then proceeded to tell Peter his testimony. He shared how his whole life had been transformed after he put his faith in Jesus Christ.

He shared how Jesus could help him to get a fresh start in life by setting him free from alcohol.

Peter found it strange that his former drinking buddy was now preaching religion to him. *He'll get over it soon enough,* thought Peter, as he listened awkwardly to his friend's mini-sermon. As soon as David was finished, Peter took the money and hurried off to drink.

Over the next ten years, Peter would visit David from time to time to ask for money. And every time, David would first preach to him before giving him any.

"Come and stay here awhile with me," David kept on urging his friend. "Jesus can straighten out your life! Why let alcohol ruin your body and soul? Come on, what do you say?"

But Peter always refused. Like many of David's former buddies, he was extremely skeptical of David's turnaround and his "Jesus talk." In the meantime, his life kept going downhill.

On a chilly morning in December 1985, ten years after he had first approached David for money, Peter was stumbling alone on the streets of Rangoon, trying to make his way to the liquor store. David happened to be riding by in a taxi with Howard and suddenly noticed him. Shocked at the sight of his friend's condition, David stopped the car immediately and hopped out.

"You look terrible!" David said to Peter. "If you continue on like this, I know you won't make it! Stop being so stubborn! Come and stay at my place for a while and get delivered from this poison!"

This time, Peter agreed to go. He had finally "hit bottom." By the age of 41, he had lost his job, his family and his health—all due to drinking and gambling. He was divorced, bankrupt, living with fellow drunkards, and on the verge of physical collapse. Knowing that he wouldn't last much longer, he finally agreed to give MYC a try.

For several weeks Peter sat attentively through sermon after sermon. For the first time in his life, he started to read the Bible. Gradually he became convinced that the gospel message was indeed for him: Jesus

MYC senior leaders ministering to new believers in Mandalay: Peter Bo (back row, third from left), Albert Howard (back row, fourth from left) and David (far right)

Christ alone had the power to save his soul and change his life. In spite of his Buddhist upbringing, he told David that he wanted to become a Christian. With great joy David counseled him, led him to the Lord, and baptized him.

Within three months, Peter was completely set free from alcohol and cigarettes. His asthma cleared up and he no longer had to use an inhaler to breathe. He was so excited about what Jesus Christ had done in his life that he couldn't wait to tell others about it. He began to join David enthusiastically in every aspect of MYC's ministry, including the gospel tours and mini-crusades. Despite being a new believer himself, he quickly became a second father to the other residents because of his age (he and David were both in their early 40s by this time) and his comparatively better educational background. David, recognizing his friend's potential as an up-and-coming MYC leader, decided to send him in 1987 to Faith Baptist Bible College (Chin State) for further training. Peter was 43 at the time.

All of David's mighty men called him "Papa," along with the rest of the MYC residents. Even Peter Bo, who was three months older than David, called him "Papa" as he also regarded David as his spiritual father. They were all greatly inspired by David's personal example of big-hearted generosity, fearless courage, and joyful sacrifice, and they all strove to develop these same qualities in their own lives. If there was no money for travel fare, they all learned—like David—to joyfully sell their own clothes (*lungis*) for the Lord. If there was no rice to eat, they all learned—like David—to joyfully fast and pray without complaining. They all prayed together, walked together, taught together, and struggled together. And through it all, David's inner circle of leaders grew strong, bold and able.

In later years, David would look back and realize that through this process, God was greatly strengthening MYC's home base in preparation for the next phase of ministry growth. In the meantime, however, no one could have predicted what would happen next.

NEVER SAY DIE

CHAPTER 11
Rocking for Jesus
(1985-1995)

"Papa! Please come quick!" shouted one of the MYC staff as he ran into David's office. "You have a special visitor: Saw Bwe Hmu!"

David jumped up to his feet. "*Saw Bwe Hmu?* You've got to be kidding!"

Saw Bwe Hmu was the nation's number one rock-and-roll guitarist, the Burmese equivalent of Elvis Presley or Jimi Hendrix. He mesmerized crowds with his matchless, super-fast finger work on the guitar. The Karen pop icon was everything one expected a top rock star to be: rough, tough and bad. He sported a rough-looking beard and grew his jet black hair down to his waist. He was also a notorious drug addict, hooked on heroin, LSD and other chemical substances. Several times he had nearly died from drug overdoses.

Always interested in the latest musical trends, David had once gone to see Saw Bwe Hmu in concert. In the middle of his performance, he suddenly hurled his guitar up towards the sky and casually walked away. To the shock of his audience, the guitar came crashing down to the ground and smashed into pieces. No one dared say anything to him, because of his stature. But people knew that years of drug use were finally taking a severe toll on his judgment and his health.

What in the world is Saw Bwe Hmu doing here? wondered David as he went out to meet him. For he knew that outside of Rangoon's Christian community, few people—let alone national celebrities—cared about or even knew much about MYC.

Upon meeting David, Saw Bwe Hmu went straight to the point. "I've come here because I want to quit drugs," he shared frankly. "I've tried everything else, but nothing has worked. The military hospital is useless: I went there for treatment, but I walked out because I couldn't handle any more of their medicines. People tell me that only God can heal me, and that's why I'm here. I want God to heal me! Can you help?"

David was stunned. He had never imagined that such a high-profile figure would ever come to MYC for treatment. Deeply humbled that the Lord was entrusting such a man into his hands, David quickly prayed for wisdom while assuring Saw that he would do all he could to help him get free from drugs.

Within a few weeks of coming to MYC in 1985, Saw Bwe Hmu had accepted the Lord and had become totally drug-free. News of his complete turnaround made national headlines. His associates in the music industry flocked to congratulate him on successfully quitting drugs. At the same time, his former contractors rushed forward to express their desire to produce his next album. It was guaranteed to be a smash hit, they said, given all the media publicity surrounding his transformation.

"Sorry, but I'm not working with any of you anymore," Saw Bwe Hmu flatly announced. "From now on, I'm only working for God!"

The music industry couldn't believe it, but it was true: the King of kings had really transformed Burma's king of rock-and-roll. Saw Bwe Hmu was so grateful for what the Lord had done in his life that he didn't even want to go back home! The only thing he wanted to do was to stay on at MYC and serve the Lord there through his music. Like the other residents, he had finally found something in David's campus that he had never experienced anywhere else—the true love of Christ.

While David was understandably thrilled that the nation's top rock musician wanted to join his ministry, he knew that it wouldn't be fair to Saw's wife and children. But when he told Saw that he needed to return home to take care of his family, he stubbornly refused to listen.

Unable to convince him any further, David decided to pay a personal visit to Saw's wife to find a workable solution.

"Don't worry about us—I don't want him back anyway!" Saw's wife muttered, obviously fed up with her husband's irresponsible behavior over the years. "In fact, please keep him with you for the rest of his life. You'll be doing me a favor!"

Once it became clear that Saw Bwe Hmu would be staying on at MYC, David's mind began to race. He, more than any other Christian leader in Burma, understood at a deep level the power that contemporary music had over the young generation. He knew that music possessed the unique power to influence for good as well as for evil.

Although David had tried his best over the past decade to offer a quality Christian alternative to secular music, he realized that his music ministry had reached a plateau. Up until then, MYC had been composing only country-jazz gospel songs. But the musical tastes of the youth were quickly switching over to rock, and so far no Christian group had dared explore this unknown territory. David desperately wanted to launch out in this area, but he needed the right person to take the lead. With Saw Bwe Hmu's arrival, David understood that God was finally throwing the door wide open for MYC to launch out in an exciting new musical direction, for the glory of God and for the evangelization of Burma.

When David returned from his next U.S. ministry visit, he brought back with him a stack of the latest American Christian rock albums: Petra, DeGarmo and Key, Amy Grant and others. He called Saw Bwe Hmu to his office and handed the albums over to him.

"Listen to this music carefully, to get an idea of how the Americans are doing Christian rock," David explained to his new disciple. "And then let's start composing our own gospel rock songs, for the glory of God!"

Saw Bwe Hmu couldn't have been happier with his new mission. Over the next decade (1985-1995) as he led MYC's music ministry, he composed numerous Burmese gospel rock songs (and later gospel heavy metal songs), many of which became nationwide hits. The songs featured gospel-centered lyrics set to pulsating, deafening rock music. Many of the songs dealt with questions that the youth wrestled with: *Who am I? Where am I going? What will happen after I die? What is the meaning of life?* The nation's youth—Buddhist and Christian alike—simply couldn't get enough of it! Saw organized these songs into five new MYC albums, which catapulted the MYC record label onto the national scene.

With David's encouragement and blessing, Saw Bwe Hmu also founded a new secular rock band—Iron Cross—which would one day become Burma's number one rock and heavy-metal band. He stacked the band with the nation's best instrumentalists, half of whom were born-again Christians. His intention was to use Iron Cross as a tool to introduce non-Christians to the gospel, as well as to generate a healthy income to support himself as well as MYC. God honored his vision: in the coming years, the Lord would use Iron Cross to draw millions of Burmese to MYC crusades all over the country.

Of course, before Saw Bwe Hmu even came to MYC, David had already been conducting MYC crusades with his team of ex-addicts and ex-alcoholics. In the beginning, David would simply set up a makeshift stage right at MYC's front gate. While he and his team performed and preached, large crowds would gather in the streets to listen. Later on, he began receiving invitations from other churches around the country to conduct the same kind of music-and-message meetings.

These crusades were unique in three ways. First, no other Christian group in Burma besides MYC dared to have a nationwide crusade ministry, for fear of having run-ins with either the military government or the Buddhist establishment. David, on the other hand, was known for being recklessly unafraid of anyone. Having led Burma's toughest street gang for years, facing the authorities was no big deal for him.

Second, MYC crusades always featured the best of contemporary music, which itself was a huge draw for a population eager for quality musical entertainment. The fact that the music happened to be Christian was irrelevant for non-believers: they just wanted to hear good music!

And third, MYC gospel presentations—often in the form of personal testimonies by ex-addicts themselves—focused heavily on the power of Jesus Christ to transform the lives of drug addicts, alcoholics, and other "sinners." In a nation where millions of people were enslaved to drugs and alcohol, such messages always deeply touched hearts. Many people would stream forward at the end of every crusade, willing to surrender their lives to Jesus in exchange for deliverance from their destructive addictions.

During the early lean years, David ran his crusade ministry on a shoestring budget. His equipment consisted of only a few acoustic guitars, several cheap amplifiers, and a rented generator. A crowd of several hundred would curiously gather round to listen, drawn by the country jazz music. Because these meetings were low-tech and low-budget, David was able to conduct an incredible 20 mini-crusades a year—once every two or three weeks! From time to time, his ministry team would run out of money for travel fare, and they would end up having to sell their own clothes to make up the difference.

But as God gradually blessed MYC's music ministry—first through the incredible success of its 1981 runaway hit album, and second through the arrival of Saw Bwe Hmu—David decided to completely revamp his crusade strategy. Rather than conducting 20 mini-crusades a year, he would concentrate instead on organizing just three or four large-scale crusades a year in the winter months. With Saw Bwe Hmu and his Iron Cross band as a sure draw, he knew it would be easy to get crowds of at least 10,000 people.

This new mass crusade strategy worked better than David had ever dreamed of. By December, the paddy (rice) crop would have been harvested, the fields would be empty, and the rural farm workers would be free. The MYC crusade team would select a huge tract of empty paddy fields in the target area, roll in with their rented trucks, and begin unloading their musical equipment on a makeshift stage. While curious villagers looked on, the MYC staff would explain that they had traveled all the way from Rangoon to stage a free, three-day Iron Cross concert and MYC crusade for all local residents. That was all the publicity they would need.

By late afternoon the next day, tens of thousands of villagers—young and old, men and women alike—would be sitting on the ground in the fields, huddled beneath colorful shawls. Many in attendance had no access to television, movies, or any other form of electronic entertainment, so this free concert would definitely be a treat for them. Moreover, with little else to do in rural Burma except work in the fields, eat, drink country liquor, and use locally-grown opium, there was no reason why anyone would choose to miss this outdoor musical extravaganza.

The MYC crusades would usually last for three days, starting each day from seven o'clock in the evening and going until midnight. For the audience, the time would fly by quickly. David would keep the flow fast-paced and interesting, with a creative mix of music (country jazz, light pop/rock, and in later years, heavy metal), preaching, and personal testimonies from ex-addicts and ex-alcoholics. While the music would definitely be the initial draw, the gospel messages would always fall on spiritually hungry and receptive hearts. The crowds would usually swell each night, as word of the crusade spread to outlying areas.

By the final night of the crusade, there would often be 50,000 to 100,000 people in the crowd, out of which several thousand would decide to leave behind their sinful lifestyles in order to start a brand new life with Jesus Christ. Whenever possible, the MYC team would distribute Bibles and gospel literature to those who were able to read, and they would encourage the new believers to start attending church locally. They would also offer a free Bible correspondence course to anyone interested.

During the daytime, David and his fellow teammates would try to visit local opium poppy field owners to challenge them to switch over to alternative cash crops like coffee or tea. Initially, most of the growers would be unconvinced. But by the end of the crusade, many would come forward and declare that they had decided to give up growing poppies. One of the greatest crusade-related experiences for David was witnessing rural families setting their entire poppy fields on fire!

The Lord uniquely blessed David with favor in the eyes of the military government, which had long since imposed a ban on all open-air meetings and public rallies. In the early years of MYC, David had little difficulty obtaining the necessary permits for his mini-crusades. Hardly anyone in Burma was doing open-air evangelism at the time, and the government considered such religious activities harmless. But later when the government realized that Buddhists were becoming Christians through these meetings, they stopped issuing the permits.

But MYC enjoyed a unique special status with the military government due to its successful drug rehabilitation work. Over the years, a number of senior government officials had quietly approached David for help in treating their drug-addicted sons. In many cases, these young men were successfully rehabilitated at MYC after surrendering their lives to Jesus Christ. These government officials didn't care that their sons had converted to Christianity, as long as they returned home alive and drug-free. As a measure of gratefulness, they began to quietly serve as MYC advocates within the military government.

Moreover, the nation's military leaders soon realized that MYC was doing a far better job at curbing drug abuse among the youth than they could ever hope to do. Trying to copy MYC's crusade approach, the government organized several "Just Say No to Drugs" mass meetings in the countryside and even advertised free rice noodles and fish curry for all who would attend. But only the elderly showed up to listen: the youth stayed home! After several failed attempts, the military government grudgingly conceded that MYC's music-and-message approach was far more effective in alerting the public to the dangers of drug abuse than its own efforts. Therefore, David was always able to secure the needed permits for his crusades despite the government ban.

God also protected MYC's crusade ministry from insurgent attacks. Roughly a quarter of Burma's land area—particularly in Kachin, Karen, Kayah and Shan States—was under the control of various armed insurgent groups. Conducting a crusade in an insurgent-controlled region was inherently full of risks. There was always the possibility of violence, either between the MYC team and the insurgents or between the military government and the insurgents. But even though other ministries shied away from these areas, David was not intimidated. He was determined to take the gospel to every corner of his nation.

"If God opens a door for us in these regions, we must go!" David exhorted his staff. "After all, they need to hear our message of hope as much as anyone else—maybe much more."

David would first dispatch scouts to these regions to make peace with the local insurgents, requesting them to allow MYC and Iron Cross to conduct a free concert and crusade in their area. Once they would agree, David would proceed as usual. In fact, most of the insurgents would end up attending the crusade. However, they were typically forbidden by their commanders to respond to the invitation at the end, lest they compromise their commitment to waging armed revolt against the Burmese government! (One insurgent privately told David that he was deeply moved by the crusade messages and vowed to go to China as a missionary once he completed his insurgent term.)

The greatest challenges, however, came neither from government officials nor from armed insurgents. Rather, they involved traveling to the crusade sites in remote hilly locations. Because huge swaths of Burma's hill states were inaccessible by motorable roads, the MYC team would travel by vehicle as far as they could go. When the road ended, they would disembark and unload all their equipment. The journey by foot through the jungle would often take four or five days. Usually they could manage to hire local bullock carts or elephants to haul in their equipment. But on some occasions, they had no choice but to carry in their instruments and personal belongings themselves.

Trekking by foot through the jungle was neither easy nor safe. The jungles were inhabited by all kinds of wild animals: elephants, monkeys, tigers, and snakes. Their fresh prints could be seen during the day; their presence could be easily heard at night. Sometimes the bullocks would suddenly stop in their tracks, having just picked up the scent where a tiger had recently crossed the trail. No amount of prodding or whipping could make them budge in such cases, so the cart driver would have to rub chili powder in their eyes to make them run ahead!

At other times, the MYC team would suddenly encounter armed insurgents, who would suspect them of being government informers. Only after David successfully convinced them that they were pastors and not spies would the insurgents let them pass through without harm.

Nights were especially difficult, as the group would attempt to sleep under trees or banana leaves. Sometimes they would hear the rattle of a poisonous snake approaching in the dark. Immediately they would switch on a flashlight, and the snake would slither away. Sometimes it would rain heavily, drenching the entire team in their sleep. Most of the time it was cold, and there would never be enough blankets to go around because the younger men would insist on giving their blankets to the older ones. Often, team members would spend the entire night shivering, praying and singing.

Food and water along the journey was also a challenge. They would drink water from the jungle streams, which sometimes made them sick with diarrhea. For food, they would manage with provisions they had brought in from the city, supplemented by jungle bananas and other wild foods. Sometimes the host church would send a "food delegation" to meet David and his teammates at the trailhead, making their journey much easier. On one occasion, a host church in Kachin State sent a party with seven days' worth of food rations to meet the team at the trailhead, because the crusade site was a seven-day jungle trek away. The rations were all conveniently packed in large banana leaves. David and the others rejoiced at this wonderful outpouring of hospitality, until they discovered what the church had packed for them to eat—frogs, snakes, rats, eels, and dogs!

The Lord miraculously protected David and his men all these years: not a single life was ever lost. Many contracted malaria and/or diarrhea along the way, but even then they had to keep on trekking. There were several accidents, including the time when their vehicle flipped over the side of a hill and rolled down to the bottom. The vehicle was crushed, but God spared the lives of the passengers.

Another challenge presented itself once the team members reached the crusade venue: adjusting to the local food. David always instructed his men in advance to eat whatever was set before them, in order to win the hearts of the people.

"When in Rome, do as the Romans do," he would explain to the newcomers. "Even the Bible tells us to be all things to all men. If you don't eat their food, they'll conclude you don't like them, and they won't welcome you for long. If you want to share the gospel among them, then you first have to let them know that you will eat their food!"

This was much easier said than done, particularly among the various hill tribes of Burma. For example, the Karen people would serve them snakes, dogs, rats, frogs, and monkeys—all usually boiled, due to the scarcity of oil. They would boil the entire dog—even the head—and serve it with the teeth grinning at them. The taste was horrible, and all the more so because they had to eat it in the presence of the grinning head. But no one could show any squeamishness at all. The Karen would also serve fresh monkey stool (boiled) as well as rat stool. Even though the MYC team felt like vomiting, they dared not show even the least bit of discomfort, lest they insult their hosts. With a "Praise the Lord!" they would quickly swallow their food with a smile.

Over time after multiple visits to these regions, David and his senior leaders eventually learned to enjoy some of these exotic foods. Most of the veteran crusaders became quite used to rat curry, dog curry, cat curry, snake curry, and lizard curry. They even concluded amongst themselves that monkey stool tasted far better than rat stool! But one food item they could never bring themselves to enjoy was the live baby rats served by the Ann people of Eastern Shan State. David and his men did eat them as a matter of principle, but they prayed they would never have to do so again!

David's Coco Island vision had finally come to pass: the vision in which he saw himself performing at an open-air concert with a gospel band, overlooking a sea of faces. He knew this didn't happen because of his own ability or effort, but only because of God's grace upon his life. Often he marveled at how God could take a drug addict like himself and use him to minister to every corner of his nation. It was only God's mercy, he knew, and this knowledge drove him to greater depths of humility and commitment.

Some older Christians questioned the direction in which David was taking his music ministry. "The youth love your music, but we can't stand the rock-and-roll!" they would complain. "You're so gifted— why don't you compose some hymns so we can also enjoy listening?"

David's answer was always the same: young people (30 and under) comprised the greatest percentage of Burma's population, so in order to reach Burma for Jesus, he had to reach the hearts of the youth. Burmese young people, Buddhist and Christian alike, all turned to music for comfort and entertainment. And unless he could produce an attractive Christian alternative, he knew they would keep on being influenced by Buddhist pop music. Hence his commitment to packaging the unchangeable message of gospel in the latest, coolest musical wrapper—whether that be country jazz, rock, or heavy metal.

With tens of thousands of people getting saved across the country, and with more and more requests for long-term help pouring in from these different regions, David realized that he needed many more trained men to handle the follow-up work. God had already blessed him over the years with a dozen or so core leaders to help him shoulder his ministry in Rangoon. But where would he find dozens more men willing and committed to provide spiritual care in these remote jungle areas?

The Lord would soon give him the answer.

NEVER SAY DIE

CHAPTER 12
Turning Lions into Lambs (I)
(1990s-2002)

"**D**id you hear about the latest crazy idea to enter David Yone Mo's brain?" asked one Yangon (formerly Rangoon) pastor to his colleague.

"You mean his new Bible school?" the other pastor queried.

"Yes, can you believe it? A Bible school for drug addicts? And led by drug addicts? That guy is out of his mind!" the pastor exclaimed. "It's one thing to help those kind of people get off drugs—that's fine. But to think that they might be fit enough to attend Bible school—well, that's downright crazy!"

The pastor paused for a moment before continuing. "And can you believe this: he actually asked me if I wanted to enroll any of my church members in his new school! Side by side with his drug addicts!"

David had known for many years that ex-alcoholics and ex-drug addicts made the boldest, most fearless and most sacrificial preachers. He had seen this in his own life. He had seen this in the lives of his leaders: Howard, Peter Bo, Peter Ling, Zaw Naw and others. He had seen this in the lives of the young men who had come to MYC and gotten off drugs through the power of Jesus Christ.

What was it about these ex-addicts that made them such fiery, dedicated preachers? For one, they understood at a deep level how wicked and sinful they were, and how much Christ had forgiven them.

"Whoever has been forgiven much, loves much," David used to remind them, quoting from the Bible. And it was true: they seemed to love Jesus Christ more than the regular church members, because they knew they had hurt Him more and had been forgiven of much more. Even though they knew that they could do nothing to earn their forgiveness, they still felt that at the very least they ought to "pay Jesus back" with love. And this "love payment" took the form of dedicated, sacrificial service. David had regularly observed that ex-addicts were much more reliable than regular believers, when it came to ministry commitment.

And second, ex-addicts knew no fear. In order to pursue their own "high," they had learned to overcome fear of their parents, fear of society and fear of the authorities. They had spent years living recklessly for themselves, so it was nothing for them to start living recklessly for the God who had delivered them. Moreover, because most addicts came from remote jungle hill states like Kachin, Chin and Shan, they were "tough" as compared to the regular "soft" urban believers. As a result, David could take them anywhere for ministry—whether on the streets or in the jungle—and he would never hear them complain about any hardship, fear or danger.

For all these reasons, David realized that the ex-addicts who were living, eating and sleeping with him represented the best pool of manpower available to meet the growing staff needs of his ministry. As MYC's crusade operations continued to expand, David needed many more faithful men who could stay behind after each crusade to do follow-up. And who better to send to these remote jungle villages than his own ex-addicts, who were not only fearless, bold and passionate, but who also in many cases were born and brought up in the same regions?

There was just one problem. The ex-addicts were eager to serve God, but they lacked adequate Bible knowledge. Before he could send any of them out on their own to do follow-up ministry—which basically meant being a pastor to the new believers—he needed to make sure that they were thoroughly grounded in God's Word. But how could he do this? The six-month Bible course he was offering was obviously not enough. What could he do to radically upgrade the quality of Bible teaching at his rehab center?

The answer came when Peter Bo arrived back from studying at Faith Baptist Bible School in 1991. He had grown by leaps and bounds during his four-year study there and had come back well-grounded in God's Word and confident in teaching it. Given his stellar academic background—he was a Rangoon University graduate—David realized that Peter was the right man to undertake this new project.

"Peter, I'd like you to completely re-do the Bible component of our rehab program," David requested. "I want to see these ex-addicts becoming pastors one day—lions becoming lambs! Let's turn our rehab center into a formal Bible school, so the ex-addicts can come out as well-equipped in God's Word as you are. From today on, you're the new principal!"

The idea seemed crazy to many people, but Peter Bo was excited by this new challenge. That same year he started the Evangelical Baptist Bible School (EBBS) at MYC. The school was affiliated with Faith Baptist Bible School (Tiddim, Chin State), which gave it credibility and accountability. The mission of the school was straightforward: to teach the Word of God faithfully and systematically over a three-year period. All residential ex-addicts would be required to enroll as part of their rehab program, and they would be awarded degrees (Bachelor's of Ministry, Graduate of Theology or Certificate in Theology) according to their academic progress. David was so confident that God would bless this new venture that he even invited other churches to send their young people to study there too. Many pastors scoffed at the thought of sending "normal" believers to study alongside drug addicts, but a few responded positively.

There were 50 students in the first batch of MYC Bible school students. Forty were residential ex-addicts and ten were outside students (male and female) from other churches. In the beginning, Peter Bo, David, Howard, and other MYC staff tried to handle the teaching load themselves. It didn't take long for them to realize that they needed extra help:

running a full-time Bible school was not easy at all! Peter soon arranged for outside teachers to come in and handle many of the academic subjects.

To everyone's surprise, the MYC Bible school flourished. God's hand of blessing was indeed upon this crazy venture. The ex-addicts thrived in this new structure and exceeded everyone's expectations in terms of their capacity to learn, study and grow. Outsiders dared not mock the school anymore, for it became apparent that the ex-addicts were just as serious about learning, if not more so, than the non-addicts. In fact, visitors to the classrooms were often unable to distinguish between the two groups. The first batch of students graduated in 1995, and they were solidly grounded in God's Word, spiritually mature, and able to preach and teach.

The following year in 1996, MYC decided to upgrade its Bible school to a Bible college. Peter Bo completely revised and strengthened the syllabus and brought in many additional outside lecturers. With this upgrade he realized that he needed more training himself, so in 1998 David sent him to Singapore to pursue a two-year master's degree. In his place, David appointed Peter Ling—who had just completed his theological studies in India—as the new principal.

Meanwhile, David had a new task on his hands: trying to figure out how to guide and direct a growing number of MYC Bible school graduates who wanted to serve the Lord full-time. Of course, this was a task he thoroughly enjoyed! Naturally, he asked each graduate to pray about his or her own future, to try to discern God's call. Most of the graduates from non-addict backgrounds wanted to go back and serve at their home churches. But most of the ex-addict graduates desperately wanted to remain with MYC and serve the Lord there. They had no desire to return home, because MYC had become their new home and family.

Some of these graduates, David realized, would make excellent MYC headquarters staff: serving with the rehab program, helping with the orphans, joining the music/crusade ministry, and working in other departments. Those who were prayerfully selected for such positions rejoiced, because they could give themselves fully to the Lord's service while still remaining under Papa's loving care. In this way, virtually all of MYC's staff continued to be comprised of either former addicts or former alcoholics—a distinctive which set MYC apart from every other ministry in the country.

But David knew that an equally important need was out in the remote villages, where there was a great deal of crusade follow-up work to be done. Would the new graduates be willing to serve in such backwards places, which usually lacked electricity, fans, air conditioners and other urban amenities?

"Sure! Send us and we will go!" responded most of the ex-addicts enthusiastically.

"Well, we need to pray about it first," the non-addict graduates from church backgrounds would usually answer half-heartedly.

David smiled. He knew that he could count on his ex-addict graduates to go where no one else wanted to go, and he had full confidence that God would bless them with fruit. If God could use a drug-addict gangster like himself, then surely He could use these ex-addicts, too. After they graduated from the program, they were kept at MYC a while longer in order to give them more practice preaching and teaching. Once David was confident that they could manage on their own, he would commission them as church planters and dispatch them to various regions across the country.

The young, fearless, ex-addict Bible graduates would be sent to various remote jungle fields where MYC had earlier conducted crusades. As part of their follow-up ministry, they would start a Bible study for anyone interested. Eventually the Bible study group would reach 20 or so members, at which time they would form a small church. Under the passionate leadership of the zealous ex-addict preachers, the MYC church plants would eventually grow to 50, 100, or even 300 members. In some places, the new churches would be comprised entirely of former Buddhists.

Every year there was a new batch of MYC Bible school graduates willing and eager to be sent out to the field. As a result, MYC's church-planting ministry grew rapidly. It quickly became apparent to David that he had a new problem on his hands: what to do with all these new churches! He was not in a position to provide spiritual oversight to a bunch of new congregations, nor was he interested in starting his own denomination. After all, God had called him to be an evangelist, not a church administrator. So David talked with his friends at the Evangelical Baptist Conference (EBC), and they gladly assumed responsibility for these new fellowships. From then on, all the new churches established through MYC would come under EBC's administrative and spiritual covering.

This unique partnership between the EBC and MYC worked well. By 2002, MYC graduates—mostly ex-addicts—had planted over 70 EBC churches in almost every state of Myanmar (the new name for Burma). The majority of these were located in backwards jungle regions, in keeping with David's philosophy of taking up those ministry tasks that no one else wanted to do. (Most typical Bible college graduates preferred to minister in urban areas, where the living standards were better and where they could enjoy a more comfortable life.) The MYC church planters became the pastors of their new churches, and the EBC would officially ordain them once they were married. After a church grew in size and was in need of more help, David would appoint a fresh graduate to go serve there as an assistant pastor. Truly, lions were being transformed into lambs, and God was getting all the glory.

Word began to spread of MYC's success in churning out top-quality Bible school graduates who could preach boldly, teach well and even plant churches. Under the leadership of Peter Ling and Peter Bo (who had since returned from Singapore), the Bible college expanded. By 2002 there were 150 students enrolled: half were ex-addicts from MYC's rehab program and the other half came from outside churches (mainly the newly-planted MYC churches in the field). The student body was diverse, mostly hailing from different hill tribes (Kachin, Kayin, Chin, Shan, Akha, Naga, Wa, Lahu), with a few from the majority Burmese community. There were 25 female students enrolled as well.

Apart from God's divine blessing and the faithful obedience of the MYC staff, there was another factor behind the explosive growth in MYC's Bible college and church-planting ministry in the 1990s. Since 1979, MYC had been receiving a limited amount of financial help from U.S.-based Christian Aid Mission, which at the time was serving as the designated channel for American contributions to MYC. But when David's main contact and friend there, Carl Gordon, left the organization to start a new ministry, Advancing Native Missions (ANM), David decided to follow suit. In 1994 he switched over his partnership to ANM, a decision which proved to be extremely beneficial in the coming years. Through ANM, the amount of American financial contributions to MYC's ministry more than quadrupled. And with these extra funds, David was able to upgrade his Bible school, support his fast-growing team, and greatly improve his ministry infrastructure.

Through MYC, God was indeed turning lions into lambs. And David was ever thankful that the Lord was allowing him to play a key role in this process.

MYC Headquarters on Insein Road, Yangon (1998)

MYC Bible College staff and students. Left of David are Albert Howard and Kevin Yone Mo; right of him are Peter Lin and Zaw Naw. (1998)

MYC Bible College students attending class (1999)

MYC gospel teams traveling by various modes of transport
to reach interior villages (1997)

David and Albert Howard visiting a newly-established
house church in a remote village (1997)

Kevin Yone Mo baptizing new believers in the field

David during his first visit to ANM, based in Virginia, U.S. (1994)

CHAPTER 13
Turning Lions into Lambs (II)
(1990s-2002)

The young addict looked extremely uncomfortable sitting in the chair, waiting to meet the director. His head was bowed and his gaze lowered. His father was sitting next to him, clearly restless and anxious.

Even though David had brought on many ex-addict Bible school graduates to assist with his drug rehab ministry, he continued to personally interview each of the new arrivals. It took only a few seconds for him to size up an addict and understand where he was coming from.

The young man sitting before him was in his early 20s. A white T-shirt and a pair of blue jeans hung loosely on his thin frame. He looked emaciated and sickly: it was obvious that he had been using drugs for many years. David also suspected that he was HIV-positive, although he would need a blood test to confirm his hunch.

"So tell me, how long have you been using drugs?" David casually asked.

"A few months," came the mumbled reply.

"Don't lie to me!" snapped David immediately. "You've been using drugs for at least five years! Snakes can see each other's legs!"

The young man suddenly became alert, having been cornered unexpectedly. By the look in his eyes, David knew he was right.

"Tell the truth, young man, and the truth will set you free." David paused for a moment before looking straight into his eyes. "Do you really want to be set free from drugs?"

The young man nodded his head.

"Well, I can't set you free. Education can't set you free. You need a change of heart—that alone will set you free," said David. "For that to happen, you'll need to stay here at least three years. During this time, we'll teach you how to change your heart."

At the mention of three years, the young man's eyes popped open wide. Three years seemed like forever to him.

"How about six months?" asked the addict's father hopefully. "I know other rehab programs run for six months. Could my son study here for six months?"

David looked at the father and answered, "If it were just six months, the whole world would be coming here. It's not about a few months of education. If you educate a thief, he won't change his way of life. He'll only become a smarter thief. What he needs is a complete change of heart. And only God can do that, but it takes time—lots of time. That's why we're different from every other rehab center."

No one could argue with David's last point. MYC was indeed different from every other drug rehab center in the country. The other government-run centers had success rates of 10% or less. But MYC boasted an incredible success rate of 80%. Most treatment centers considered their clients successfully rehabilitated as long as they stopped using illegal drugs. For them, continued alcohol and cigarette use was acceptable. But MYC held to much stricter standards: for David, success meant no more drugs, no more alcohol, and no more smoking!

By the 1990s, MYC's extraordinarily high success rate had become well-known throughout Myanmar. Of course, David and his staff knew fully well that this was entirely due to the program's emphasis on Jesus Christ and His power to deliver and transform.

But Buddhist and secular observers tended to attribute MYC's success to other reasons. One was that nearly all of MYC's program staff were ex-addicts who had gone through the same program themselves. Another was that MYC's staff clearly possessed an unusual, loving concern for each of the residents, as opposed to simply doing their jobs for pay. This kind of faithful and loving dedication could not be easily reproduced elsewhere.

Over time MYC began attracting addicts from the most unlikely backgrounds and places. Some, like rock-and-roll icon Saw Bwe Hmu, left government rehab centers to join MYC's program. Buddhist monks, police officers, and children of drug czars all showed up, humbly asking for help in overcoming their shameful addictions. Even senior government ministers and military colonels sent their own sons to MYC for treatment. None of these families cared if their sons ended up becoming Christians after coming to MYC. For them, they would rather have their sons become drug-free Christians than remain as drug-addicted Buddhists!

News of MYC's exceptional work also spread internationally. Foreign news media from Japan, Thailand, and the Philippines came to conduct interviews, and soon articles about MYC were being written up in the Nippon Post, Bangkok Post and the Manila Chronicle. Several Asian television networks aired special features about MYC's unusual approach to drug rehabilitation. The United States government praised MYC's unique role in combating drug abuse in the heart of the Golden Triangle region, and its government invited David to visit the U.S. on two separate occasions for official drug rehabilitation and narcotics work. The German Embassy in Yangon awarded David a silver medal for exemplary social work.

And last but not least, even the United Nations (UN) took note of MYC's work. The UN Development Program office in Myanmar had been working to stem the rising tide of drug abuse in the country. It didn't take long for them to recognize that MYC's two-pronged approach—prevention through education (the crusade ministry) and treatment through rehabilitation—was yielding far better results than any other program in the country. After visiting MYC and taking a closer look at the organization's work, they invited David to their Yangon office for official talks.

"We recognize and salute the amazing social work being done by your organization, in terms of drug abuse prevention and treatment," the UN officials candidly told David. "And we would be honored to come alongside you, to help you accomplish your objectives."

David's ears perked up. *Was this for real? Would the UN really help MYC?*

"The UN has a significant budget for social work in Myanmar, especially in the area of drug abuse prevention and treatment," the officials continued. "We can make available to you whatever financial help you need. There's just one small thing that we need to address, though."

"What's that?" asked David.

"The UN is not authorized to fund religious programs. But we're very much interested and willing to fund social work. If you can modify your program just a bit by removing the religious component, then your organization will meet all our criteria, and you will qualify to receive UN funds."

David tensed up. He didn't like the sound of this at all.

"I'm sorry," he interrupted, "but there's no need to continue this discussion. I'm not interested in doing social work. I'm interested in pointing these addicts to Jesus Christ, who alone can deliver them from their addictions. If Jesus Christ is not in the picture, then I'm afraid there is no picture at all!"

The UN officials were stunned. How could David be so foolish as to turn down their financial aid? But David knew better than to compromise. He knew that the Lord had brought MYC thus far without UN help, and He would surely provide for them in the coming days as well.

For many years, the quarter-acre MYC compound in the heart of Yangon had been bursting at the seams with drug addicts, orphans, rock musicians and Bible college students—all living, working, eating and sleeping together with David's own family. Most of the time it felt like a zoo, but David and Kathy had earlier made a commitment to endure everything joyfully for the Lord. Even so, they had long dreamed of having a separate campus to house the drug addicts and Bible college students. It would give them and the rest of the MYC family much more badly needed space.

The Lord answered their prayers in 1998 when MYC was able to purchase a huge five-acre plot of land in Hmawbi, located 30 miles north of Yangon. The site was perfect: spacious enough to build David's dream rehabilitation center, while close enough to be within a reasonable drive from MYC headquarters.

Construction of the new Hmawbi campus went very quickly. Most of the funding came from American donors through ANM. The five-acre plot was divided into two parts by a road. On one side was the drug rehabilitation center, and on the other side was the Evangelical Baptist Bible College. David constructed men's and women's dormitories, classrooms, offices, staff quarters, a huge kitchen and dining hall, an 800-seater church with a library on top, and even a fish pond. Never in his wildest dreams did he imagine that God would bless MYC with such wonderful facilities. With the additional space at Hmawbi, MYC would now be able to accommodate up to 100 residential male ex-addicts at a time. (Most of the time, the number of residents would hover between 70 and 80, which was ideal.) In addition, there was room for another 100 regular (non-addict) Bible college students. The campus was ready for occupancy by 1999 and dedicated that same year.

In 2002, MYC started two additional smaller drug rehab centers in the cities of Kalemyo and Tamu (both in Sagaing Division in northwest Myanmar), after conducting hugely successful crusades there. A combined total of nearly 60,000 people had stood up to accept Christ on the final night when the invitation was given, out of which many were hard-core drug addicts. Realizing the impracticality of trying to bring hundreds more addicts across the country to Yangon, David and the other MYC senior staff were led to start new rehab centers in each of these cities. This brought the total number of MYC drug rehabilitation centers to three.

By the early 1990s, after almost two decades of trial-and-error experience, MYC had finally developed a successful model for drug rehabilitation that would only need minor adjustments in the years to come. The first order of business was always interviewing the new arrivals. They were usually in their 20s and hooked on a lethal combination of heroin, opium and other chemical substances. David and other senior staff members would first ask each one if he sincerely wanted to get off drugs. If he had come only because his family was pushing him—as was often the case—then there was no point in continuing any further.

Once it became clear that the addict himself really wanted to quit drugs, then the staff would carefully explain to him the rules and regulations. Addicts would be required to stay for a minimum of three years. During that time they would not be allowed to return home, but they could receive visits from relatives. This was for their own good, because experience had proven that residents who returned home before completing the program usually relapsed after meeting old friends.

Residents would be required to strictly follow all the rules, including no drugs, no alcohol, no cigarettes, no sex and no violence. The first time a resident broke a rule, his head would be shaved—which would significantly embarrass the offender, according to Burmese culture. If he broke the rules a second time, he would be expelled.

Residents would also be required to attend daily devotions, Bible studies and Bible classes, regardless of their religious background. However, they would not be pressured or forced to become Christian. Most of the new arrivals came from nominal Christian backgrounds (Kachin, Chin, Karen), so they had no problem with this requirement. Those from Buddhist and Muslim backgrounds also generally had no difficulty with this, as long as they were desperate enough to get off drugs.

After listening to the MYC policies, typically half of the new arrivals—those who were not very serious about quitting—would decide not to go through with the program. The other half would pledge to abide by the terms and conditions. At this point, the MYC staff would conduct a thorough search of their bags and bodies. Often they would find drugs cleverly stashed in their shoes, belts, collars, jackets, medicine bottles, and even underpants! Being ex-addicts themselves who had practiced these same tricks in the past, the staff could not be fooled.

The first week would be the most difficult period for the new arrivals, because of the withdrawal symptoms. Typically the severe withdrawal period would last four to five days, during which time they would be unable to eat or sleep properly. The staff would ask them to take lots of showers and pray fervently for them. Most addicts would feel like giving up and going back home, but the staff would constantly counsel them, pray with them, and motivate them to keep on going.

"You've been thinking only about yourself all this time," the staff would say. "You need to start thinking about your family! Think about your parents and your brothers and sisters. By staying here, you're actually doing a favor to your family!"

After two or three weeks, the addict would slowly begin to settle into his new way of life at Hmawbi. When the Bible college was in session, he would attend classes during the day and study in the evening. When the college was on break, he would spend his days with the other program residents studying the Bible, memorizing Scripture verses, doing campus chores, playing sports and attending worship services. Daily interaction with the staff and other residents would be the best source of inspiration for him, as he would slowly realize that it was indeed possible—with God's help—to start a brand new life.

Within six months, the new arrival would have put on weight and looked much better than when he arrived. The food at Hmawbi was good: David always made sure they had a balanced, nutritious diet, including regular meat. The combination of disciplined study, exercise, daily chores and social interaction helped to create in each resident a new sense of physical, mental and emotional well-being. By this time, the craving for drugs and alcohol would have largely disappeared, although he could be easily tempted to relapse if he left MYC prematurely.

But most significantly, the new arrival would have encountered at MYC something he had never seen anywhere else: the power of Jesus Christ to transform lives and hearts. Not only was this message communicated daily through the devotional messages and Bible studies, but it was also modeled round-the-clock by each of the MYC staff and many of the senior residents. Regardless of his religious background, no new arrival could escape the fact that Jesus Christ had truly transformed the lives of many hard-core addicts. As a result, within their first six months, most residents would have voluntarily chosen to surrender their hearts to Jesus Christ, asking Him to do the same transforming work in their messed-up lives.

Typically around 80% of incoming residents would end up completing MYC's three-year program and graduate successfully, having lost all desire to smoke, drink, or use drugs again. All graduates would have become genuine born-again Christians at some point during their stay, regardless of their previous religious background.

Upon graduating, most of the residents would not want to leave. They would have found at MYC a new brotherhood, a new family, a new Lord and a new way of life, and they would have no desire to return to their former dead-end environments. About 25% would be obligated to return home to help with the family business, but even then they would try to attend a local MYC church if possible and stay connected to the ministry in some way. The other 75% would decide to serve the Lord, either at MYC headquarters or in the field. This was a good thing, as David knew that serving the Lord was the best way to prevent future relapse.

Upon graduating, residents were also free to do something else: pursue girls. While an addict was using drugs, he would have no interest at all in the opposite sex. But once he became drug-free, his feelings for girls would begin to stir. These feelings were often reciprocated: many Christian girls intentionally came to the MYC church just to meet Christian boys, having found the boys in their own churches to be sorely lacking in spiritual zeal as compared to the ex-addicts.

MYC regulations strictly prohibited all boy-girl relationships during the program. "If you focus on girls, you'll not focus on Bible study!" David would warn. Boys and girls were together in the Bible college and at church, but they were not permitted to speak to each other in private. After graduating, however, the young men were free to court the girls, and often they would end up marrying.

Outsiders marveled at how MYC could transform wild drug addicts into devout preachers in just three years—"lions into lambs." Of course, David knew that it was entirely because of the program's focus on Jesus Christ as the sole source of deliverance, healing and empowerment for godly living. But there was another reason too: the matchless dedication of David's staff. Led by his son Kevin, whom he had appointed as director over the drug rehab ministry at Hmawbi, his team of devoted staff faithfully carried out the ministry's vision and values.

Although he was not an ex-addict himself, Kevin Yone Mo had lived with drug addicts and alcoholics his whole life. Up until age eight, he had seen how his father had acted before he became drug-free. And after his father's conversion, he had shared a house with the addicts and drunkards whom his father had brought home to rehabilitate. Growing up in this environment, Kevin had long since learned all the ins and outs of an addict's life: his cravings, tricks and patterns of behavior. As such, he was uniquely suited to oversee this type of ministry.

Aside from his son Kevin, virtually all the rest of the staff were ex-addicts who had graduated from MYC's program. As a result, each one could identify personally with the residents' feelings, thoughts and struggles. Each one had surrendered his heart to Jesus Christ after coming to MYC, whether hailing from a nominal Christian, Buddhist or Muslim background. And each one was deeply committed to working and praying for the success of the new arrivals.

Over the years, hundreds of lions were transformed into lambs through MYC's drug rehab ministry. La Tawng was a typical example. A Kachin from Shan State, he had started using drugs and alcohol from age 15. He quickly became addicted; and in order to fund his expensive drug habit, he left home for Kachin State to dig jade. After four years of drug use, he became disgusted with his way of life and wanted to quit, but he did not know how.

One day La Tawng heard someone from his village sharing his testimony about how God had transformed his life at a place called MYC. Desperate to be set free himself, he traveled to Yangon for the first time in 1995 and admitted himself at MYC. The first two months were terrible due to his withdrawal symptoms, and he could not sleep properly at all. But the love of the staff and the other residents sustained him through that difficult period. Daily he heard the gospel being preached, and slowly its message took root in his heart. Although he had been baptized many years earlier, he had no idea at the time what it meant. Only after coming to MYC did he understand that Jesus Christ had already died for his sins, and that in response he ought to live his life for Him.

In 1998 he tested positive for AIDS. Even so, he was not shaken: he had by now come to understand that the disease was a result of his own sin and that his life was now in God's hands. Upon graduating in 1999, he told David that he wanted to stay on and serve the Lord there.

"Papa, unless I live for God, I have no reason to live," he expressed frankly. "I know it takes ex-addicts to help other addicts, and I wish to be a counselor here to help others—if you would let me!"

David agreed to let La Tawng stay on as a rehab counselor at Hmawbi. La Tawng was delighted: he would finally have a chance to do something for the God who had delivered him from the curse of drugs. For La Tawng, living with AIDS was not a sign of shame. Rather, it made him all the more determined to live every day for the Lord.

Hein Htaik Thaw was another example of a lion-turned-lamb. A Burmese Buddhist, he joined a Yangon street gang called the Scorpions and quickly became hooked on drugs. His mother was alarmed by his addiction and tried various ways to get him to quit, but without any success. At one point she even sent him to a Buddhist monastery to become a monk, but after two weeks he couldn't handle the withdrawal symptoms and ran away. In desperation she contacted the UN Development Program office in Yangon for suggestions, and they told her about MYC. Even though she was Buddhist, she convinced her son to give the Christian rehab center a try.

Hein was admitted to MYC in 1999. Initially he didn't like the program at all: there were far too many rules and regulations, and he had no interest in the Bible lessons. But every time he thought about leaving, he remembered that the police were still out to arrest him because of his gang involvement. As a result, he forced himself to stay.

Gradually the Word of God convicted his heart, and after eight months Hein decided to become a Christian. The Lord delivered him from all his addictions and filled him with a new joy. His mother didn't mind that he had become a Christian, so long as he was drug-free and well-behaved. In 2002 he graduated from the Bible college and told David that he would like to continue serving there.

"Papa, I know it was God's plan for me to come to MYC. In this place he saved me from my sin, He saved me from drugs, and He saved me from police arrest. I'd like to serve Him the rest of my life!" Hein expressed.

Upon graduation Hein also joined the staff of the Hmawbi campus, helping to look after the new arrivals and other residents. He went back to his old gangster friends and shared his testimony with them. In the process, he managed to convince three of them to enroll at MYC to clean up their lives. Hein also became a frequent speaker at MYC functions, sharing his testimony of God's transforming work in his life. In his testimony he would share that when he first came to MYC, he tested positive for HIV. But after graduating from the program, his blood tests repeatedly came out negative for HIV—further proof of God's merciful healing hand in his life!

David knew that God had given him a unique calling to minister to drug addicts. In twenty-five years' time, he had watched the Lord gradually transform MYC from a group of rowdy addicts sleeping and vomiting on the floor of his own home to an internationally-recognized drug rehabilitation center. Nothing gave him more satisfaction than knowing that God had chosen him to turn lions into lambs for God's kingdom.

But even though his hands were already full, God had even more in mind for him. As always, David could never have guessed whom else the Lord would bring across his path to love and serve.

Drug addicts from rural villages being newly admitted as MYC residents, standing with a MYC drug rehab counselor (third from right) (1997)

MYC residents (recovering addicts and alcoholics) relaxing
in the drug rehab center (1998)

MYC's Hmawbi campus houses the drug rehabilitation center
as well as the Bible college (1999)

A MYC resident shares his testimony at an anti-drug abuse rally (1999)

David working in his office at MYC headquarters (1997)

CHAPTER 14
Touching the Lepers
(1984-2002)

On a hot and dusty day in 1984, a visitor walked into the MYC compound for the first time. He looked terrible: his nose and his fingertips were missing, and his skin was covered with open sores. A swarm of buzzing flies followed him in.

He was a leper.

Even the drug addicts, who were accustomed to seeing people at their worst, recoiled in disgust when they saw his condition. Most had never seen a leper before: lepers were social outcasts in Burma, forcibly banished to live in isolated colonies. Everyone knew that lepers were contagious, so they wanted them to live as far away from society as possible.

One of the ex-addicts who had just recently accepted Jesus Christ into his life looked over at David worriedly.

"Papa," he said quietly, "I know you have a good heart. I know if that poor fellow begs, you'll end up taking him in. But please don't mix lepers with drug addicts here!"

"Let's see what he has to say first," David answered cautiously. He looked at the leper with a mixture of shock and curiosity.

The visitor spoke up. "I haven't eaten for four days. Can someone give me some food?"

There was an awkward pause. Everyone waited anxiously to see how David would respond.

"Sure, I can give you some food, and it will satisfy you for a few hours. But I can also introduce you to someone who can give you food that will satisfy you forever," David answered.

The leper's eyes opened wide. "Yes, please tell me who he is!"

David then proceeded to share the gospel with the man, who was a Buddhist. It was the first time he had ever heard about Jesus, and he listened politely. David then ordered a plate of food to be brought to him. When he had finished eating, David asked him about his life.

The leper's name was Saw Nay Htoo. He had come from the government-established leper colony at Htauk Kyant, located 15 miles outside the city. There were 3,000 other lepers staying there, all living in terrible poverty. They were discouraged from venturing into the city, but on that day he had decided to go begging in Yangon.

As David listened to the man, his heart was stirred with compassion. "Can I come with some of my friends to visit and pray for you?"

The leper was taken aback by the offer. Nobody from the outside world ever wanted to visit their colony. "Of course," he answered hesitantly, suspecting that David was only trying to be polite.

David fixed a date for his visit and assured the leper that he would come. After the man left, David turned to the others and said, "Years ago I promised the Lord that I would take up those ministries that no one else wanted to do. That's why I'm helping each one of you here!"

He paused for a moment before continuing. "In the same way, I believe that God sent that leper here today for a purpose. I know what each one of you must be thinking. But let's all try to have the heart of Jesus!"

Privately, David wondered if he had made the right decision by promising to visit the leper colony. *What am I getting myself into?* he wondered. *Lord, You know my hands are full already, with all the addicts and the orphans. Did I speak too hastily?*

But when David returned to his office, his eyes fell upon the words engraved upon his wooden desk ornament: *Give me this mountain*

(Joshua 14:12). He suddenly remembered why he had chosen to keep this on his desk—as a reminder that many years ago, he had asked the Lord to give him mountains, meaning those ministries that nobody else wanted to do. He had asked for mountains, and now the Lord was giving him one. So why was he complaining?

Forgive me, Lord! he prayed with a smile.

David had never visited a leper colony before, and he certainly had reservations about going, but he was determined to keep his word. He decided to take a few of his up-and-coming leaders along with him. None of them wanted to go, but David didn't give them a choice.

When the MYC team finally reached the leper colony, they were unprepared for what they saw. Thousands of lepers were living in squalid, inhuman conditions. Most of them had open, fly-ridden sores; some even had maggots crawling on them. The stench from the open sores was absolutely revolting. Even David had a hard time masking his nausea. But they all pretended as if everything were normal.

Saw Nay Htoo was thrilled to see David and his men. Hardly anyone from the outside world had ever set foot in the colony, so it was a real honor for him to be receiving visitors. Immediately he led the MYC team into a small hut, where 15 other lepers were sitting on the floor.

"I told them you would be coming, so they've been eagerly waiting for you," Saw Nay Htoo explained.

It was summer, and there was hardly any ventilation in the room. The heat inside was oppressive, and so was the smell. David sat down and looked over his audience. The first thing he noticed was the missing noses, deformed faces, and chewed-up fingers and toes. Once again his heart was overcome with compassion.

After introducing himself and his companions, David began to share a simple gospel message about Christ's love. "God really does love each one of you!" He went on to talk about the cross and the blessings which Jesus freely gives to all who put their faith in Him. As he spoke, the Buddhist lepers listened intently. When he had finished speaking, he prayed a short prayer of blessing over them all.

Saw Nay Htoo then announced that the women had prepared some light refreshments. Immediately David and his men tensed. If they ate the food, they could easily get sick themselves. But if they refused to eat, they would be insulting their hosts. What should they do?

Before they had time to think through this dilemma, the women had already brought out plates topped with a jelly-like dessert and laid them on the floor in front of the visitors. Flies were flitting back and forth between the food and the open sores: the sight was absolutely sickening. But David and his men knew they had no choice but to eat. After delivering a message about God's love, they would surely be watched to see whether they practiced what they preached.

David bowed his head to pray and asked the Lord to be with them as they partook of the food. The men ate quickly before any more flies could land on their plates, and they were careful not to express even a hint of squeamishness. When they were finished, the women served them more refreshments with their leprosy-ravaged finger stubs—pickled tea leaves with garlic and sesame. The MYC brothers smiled appreciatively, prayed silently, and ate that too. All this time, they were very much aware that the lepers were carefully studying them.

When they had finished eating, they saw that the lepers were delighted, because no outside guests had ever eaten their food! They invited David to come back again and share more with them, which he agreed to do. As he and his men stood up to leave, the lepers extended their arms to shake hands with them. Even though their hands were sticky and covered with oozing sores, David and his men pretended not to notice and shook them warmly.

David and his MYC brothers started visiting the Htauk Kyant leper colony every two weeks. And each time, the lepers tested the sincerity of their visitors' love by serving them food and extending their arms to shake hands. After five such visits, Saw Nay Htoo and three other lepers finally became convinced that David's message about Jesus' love was real. They told David that they wanted to become Christians, so he led them in the sinners' prayer and baptized them.

A few months later, 28 more lepers decided to become Christians and were baptized. Soon a third group of 45 followed their example. David organized the new believers into MYC's first leper church and began sending one of his key leaders to preach there every week.

The new Christian lepers faced stiff persecution from the others in the colony. The reason was because nearly all of them had been selling home-made liquor for a living. The other lepers grew suspicious when David started visiting the colony regularly, wondering if he would interfere with their illegal business. As more and more lepers started to follow Jesus, David explained to them that the liquor business was displeasing to God and therefore as Christians they should stop engaging in it. Although he had no intention of interfering with the Buddhist lepers' business, this was enough to make them feel threatened.

The Buddhist lepers began to throw stones at Saw Nay Htoo, accusing him of bringing in outsiders to destroy their way of life. They drove him out of the colony, and he had to sleep under the open sky for several days. When David learned about this, he went and brought Saw back to Htauk Kyant and reassured the Buddhist lepers that he had no intention of disturbing their way of life. For the time being, there was a temporary peace between the two groups in the colony.

In the meantime, David knew that he had to do something to help the Christian lepers, who had given up their livelihood in obedience to God's Word. MYC began supplying them with rice and vegetables on a monthly basis, as well as helping them with several income-generating projects such as planting fruit trees.

In 1989 the government suddenly decided to shift the Htauk Kyant leper colony further away to a jungle area called Myanchaung. Located 50 miles north of Yangon, Myanchaung was even more remote and desolate than Htauk Kyant. With no public transportation going there, the lepers would now be literally cut off from the rest of the world.

The place was also infested with malaria-carrying mosquitoes. Hundreds of lepers died shortly after reaching there.

Now that it would take much longer to travel to the leper colony, David decided to appoint a full-time pastor to live at Myanchaung and look after the believers. Amazingly, one of the MYC residents, Saw Htoo, volunteered to serve in this capacity—even though it meant possibly contracting leprosy himself. Saw had been inspired by David's own example of sacrificial service and was eager to lay down his life for the Lord, if necessary.

But even after appointing a full-time pastor for the leper church, David remained committed to personally visiting Myanchaung every few weeks. As no buses went that way, he and his companions would walk for two hours in either dusty heat (summer) or thick mud (rainy season) to get there. A visit to Myanchaung also meant spending the night in a malaria zone, which in turn meant sleeping on the lepers' contaminated beds. But after praying about these matters, David and his MYC brothers resolved to endure everything joyfully without complaint for the sake of the leper souls.

"If Jesus was willing to suffer for us, then we ought to be willing to suffer a little bit for Him," David told his men.

As the Buddhist lepers began to see the love of Christ lived out month after month, more and more decided to join the young leper church. After all, nobody else from the outside world had ever been willing to eat their food, shake their hands, or sleep on their beds— three things which communicated true love and acceptance to them.

As the number of believers grew, David began to help them in many practical ways. He purchased 15 acres of land for them to settle on and cultivate. With a view to helping them become economically self-sufficient, he purchased bullocks, chickens, and goats for them and also had two ponds dug so they could start breeding fish. He bought many different kinds of fruit trees for them to plant: cashew nut, guava, mango, and jackfruit. On top of all this, he would always bring extra provisions whenever he would visit, such as sacks of rice or dried fish.

Papa David getting a warm welcome from the children of the
Myanchaung leper colony (1996)

David eating a meal at the Myanchaung leper colony (1997)

The believers at the MYC Myanchaung leper colony church (1999)

David with the pastor and other leaders of the MYC Myanchaung
leper colony church (2000)

These acts of charity began to arouse jealousy among the Buddhist lepers, who plotted to destroy the new Christian community. One day they intentionally set fire to the Christian homes, leaving them half-burned. Then they filed a case against the entire Christian community, charging them with careless behavior. They were hoping that the judge would find the Christians guilty of negligent living and thus order the whole community to be disbanded. But the Lord miraculously intervened on the side of the Christian lepers: the judge who presided over the case turned out to be a personal friend of David's. As a result, David was able to explain the whole situation to the judge and thereby have the case dismissed.

In spite of such opposition, the leper church continued to grow to nearly 300 members. In response, David appointed several more full-time MYC staff to work among them. He would regularly send Bible college students there to preach God's Word and to teach them new songs. Once in a while he would even bring the MYC Praise Band to stage a gospel music rally for the entire colony.

Over time, the Buddhist lepers realized that MYC's compassionate outreach at Myanchaung brought huge benefits for the entire community. Several times a year, David would treat the entire colony to a lavish feast, purchasing 300 pounds of rice and 100 pounds of pork for them to enjoy. From time to time, David would undertake various social welfare projects in the colony, such as donating a generator for the school building or installing a new water pump. In fact, MYC's active involvement in social welfare activities at Myanchaung eventually forced the government to pay attention to their dire needs. As an example, the government entered into an agreement with MYC to pay for half the expenses of laying underground electrical cables to reach Myanchaung, with the agreement that MYC would pay for the other half.

The Myanchaung church eventually sent out a missionary pastor to another leper colony in Sagaing, north of Mandalay. Kya Shin, a leper who had accepted Jesus Christ at Myanchaung, felt a strong burden to take the gospel to other lepers who had never heard. With MYC's blessing and assistance, he moved to the Sagaing leper colony and in time established MYC's second leper church there.

Truly it could be said that over the years, those who ministered to the lepers benefited as much as the lepers themselves, because the Lord used this ministry to challenge them to a much higher level of spiritual commitment. The leper ministry also proved to be the source of endless anecdotes, some poignant and some hilarious.

For example, a group of MYC senior staff visited the Myanchaung church during Christmas 2001. In typical fashion, the leper church members cooked pork curry to celebrate the occasion. The pastor waited till all were served before he sat down to eat. In the middle of his meal, he found a gauze bandage in the curry. Tossing it to the side, he continued eating until he came across a rotten human finger mixed in with the pork.

By that point, everyone had already finished eating and was commenting on how wonderful the meal had been. The pastor quietly went to the kitchen to find out whose finger had fallen off. It didn't take long before he identified the source.

"How could you let your finger fall off into the curry?" the pastor asked the main cook.

"I'm truly sorry about that, Pastor," replied the cook, who was thoroughly embarrassed. "It must have fallen off while I was stirring the pork. I felt no pain, so I didn't know when it happened. By the time I realized my finger was gone, the food had already been served and I couldn't say anything!"

The pastor sighed but understood. Having worked with lepers for many years, he was used to such bizarre incidents. Returning to the fellowship area, he was met by the MYC senior staff.

"The meal was wonderful!" they exclaimed. "Your church members did a wonderful job preparing this feast. And the pork curry was especially delicious!"

"Ah yes, praise the Lord!" answered the pastor awkwardly. "Praise the Lord indeed!"

CHAPTER 15
Embracing More Outcasts
(1985-2002)

It was a hot and humid afternoon, and David was feeling a bit sleepy. Thinking he would lie down for a short nap, he walked out of his office, strode across the MYC compound to his house, and trudged upstairs to his bedroom.

Where is everyone? he wondered. The house was strangely quiet. Then suddenly he remembered: Kathy had taken the orphan children—nearly 20 of them—to the zoo on a special excursion.

David lay down to rest, but he could not relax. *Something is not right*, he thought to himself. But what was it? He continued to toss and turn, but still sleep would not come.

After a while, he heard the sound of many little voices outside. *They're all back*, he thought to himself. Within seconds, the noise of twenty children excitedly pushing and shoving their way up the stairs filled the house. As the children continued to chatter and make their usual commotion, David began to relax. *That was it: it was too quiet for me to sleep!* he realized. Soothed by the noisy energy, he fell fast asleep in a matter of minutes.

Outsiders had a difficult time understanding how David could handle so many orphan children living with him in his own house. But in reality, he had very little to do with taking care of them, as he was away much of the time. It was Kathy who took all the responsibility for the orphan children. Few realized what a heavy load she gladly and willingly bore, as an expression of her commitment to the Lord.

Initially they had agreed to take in only Peter Ling and his younger brother, Ma Na Kee. Then Kathy decided to accept an infant abandoned by its mother. Then Samuel and his siblings came along, and she brought them into her house too. And then another, and then another...

Eventually whenever a needy child came across their path, David would be quick to predict what Kathy's response would be. Trying to discourage her from taking in any more orphans, he would say to her, "God has already blessed us with five children of our own! Why do you want more?"

But Kathy just couldn't say no, when it came to helping needy children. A number of them came from broken homes: their parents had remarried, and they were viewed as "unwanted baggage" by their new step-parents. Others whose parents had died had been passed around from one relative to another, none of whom who were willing to take responsibility for them. Some orphans came to MYC through the crusade ministry, as poor villagers would bring needy children to the visiting MYC teams. Others came through word of mouth, as ex-addicts would return home and share about MYC's orphan ministry to their fellow villagers.

Kathy's heart would always be moved to compassion whenever she came across an orphan in need. And somehow, she always managed to persuade David to let her take in "just one more." Before long, she had brought a total of 20 orphans into their home, including Silas, Naomi, Naw Shee, Mary, Paul, Peter #2, Paul #2, Amen, Ko Htwe, Zar Chee, Po Hkwar Lay, D Gar Mo, John, Maung Aung, Mu Wah, and Da Eh.

These orphans came from various ethnic backgrounds, including Burmese, Chin, Mon, Rakhine and Wa. Many came in as Buddhists but quickly accepted the Lord after experiencing the love of Christ through Papa David and Mama Kathy. For her, the orphan ministry was a "Timothy ministry" —raising children who would grow up knowing and serving the Lord, like the Timothy of the Bible. This was in contrast to her husband's "Paul ministry" —dramatically reshaping the lives of men who had come to know Christ later in life, like the Apostle Paul.

Caring for more than 20 kids was not an easy task for Kathy, particularly as David was often away from home doing ministry. Every day she would get up at 5:00 a.m. and take the older orphan children with her to the market to buy fresh vegetables and meat. After returning home, she would begin to cook for a battalion: the 25 in her own family plus the ex-addict residents—a total of 100 people. In fact, she would spend the better part of each day in the kitchen, as there were two large meals of rice and curry to prepare for all. Of course, there were many hands around to help, but she was always the central figure in the kitchen.

By 6:00 pm everyone would have been fed twice and her kitchen duties would be over for the day. Then Kathy would sit down to lead evening devotions for the children, help them with their homework, and finally prepare them for bed. At night the children would spread out mats on the floor to sleep, four or five to a room. Only then would she have a few moments to herself, before collapsing in bed.

The Lord gave Kathy supernatural grace for many years to manage the entire household alone and keep everyone on schedule. With so many kids in the house, it was always noisy. One child would be crying; and when he stopped, another would start up. But David and Kathy quickly became accustomed to the noise. In fact, David got to the point where he couldn't sleep properly if it was too quiet in the house!

However, David and Kathy found that they could not stop at just 20 orphans. People kept on bringing children in desperate conditions to MYC's doorstep, and Kathy found it incredibly hard to turn them away. Moreover, once the leper ministry got underway, David realized that there were many healthy children born to leper parents who needed to be kept separate from their families. Otherwise, if they continued growing up with their parents in the leper colony, they would eventually contract the disease themselves.

But what could they do? Their house was already packed with children, and the rest of the tiny MYC campus was packed with ex-addicts. The only place where David could think of keeping the additional children was on the 15-acre plot of land which he had previously purchased for the Myangchaung lepers. To be sure, the location was not ideal: it was too close to the leprosy colony and too far from Yangon.

"But it will have to do for now," David said to Kathy. "We don't really have any other choice. At least there the children will get shelter, food, and clothing. And I'll make sure the lepers don't come near, for the sake of the children's health."

After much prayer concerning this matter, David decided to go ahead and construct MYC's first children's home at Myanchaung. He fenced off a portion of the 15-acre plot, turning it into a "safe zone" where the lepers would not be able to enter. Then he constructed several bamboo dormitories within the fenced enclosure. Soon 40 children were shifted to the new children's home. Most of them came from the Myanchaung leper colony itself—children born to leper parents who had not contracted leprosy themselves. Others were brought there from the outside, because Kathy had no more room for additional orphans in her house.

But David knew that the Myanchaung home was just a temporary arrangement until a suitable parcel of land could be found for a much larger, permanent orphanage. Requests to accept more orphans kept pouring in, especially from the border states where many of the MYC crusades were held. As a result, David and Kathy grew increasingly desperate for a new piece of land.

In 1994 a medical doctor at Rangoon General Hospital whose son was set free from drugs at MYC donated nearly three acres of land to the ministry out of gratitude. The land was located in Thanlyin, 18 miles south of Yangon. Initially, David had planned to build MYC's new drug rehab center and Bible college there and had even begun construction work on the site. But he later changed his mind in 1998, when the much larger plot of land at Hmawbi became available for the same purpose. As a result, the Thanlyin property became free to use for the orphanage. With assistance from ANM donors, MYC was quickly able to complete construction of its first permanent orphanage that same year.

The Thanlyin orphanage was a dream come true for MYC. With its large, spacious, separate dormitories for boys and girls, it could accommodate up to 100 orphans. Soon after it opened, the orphanage was filled to capacity. Approximately half of them were the children of Myanchaung lepers, who were shifted over to the new site. The others came from all over Myanmar, including some of the orphans who had been staying at MYC headquarters. The orphans ranged in age from two to seventeen. David appointed dedicated Christian staff to care for them, mostly ex-addicts who had graduated from MYC.

Another blessing of the Thanlyin orphanage was that there was a government school nearby. All the children could now attend school, and MYC provided them with the needed uniforms, books, and school supplies. David even sent MYC's new crusade bus to Thanlyin to transport the children to school every day, as long as there were no crusades happening.

Over the years, the Lord gave David and Kathy the joy of seeing several of their orphan children grow up to become godly adults. The eldest, Peter Ling, became one of David's right-hand men in MYC and served as the principal of the Bible college. His younger brother, Ma Na Kee, became a MYC pastor as well as the overseer of all MYC's churches. Other children like Samuel, John and Paul went on to study at the university and at the same time helped out with computer work, driving, and taking care of the younger orphans. Some of them decided to enroll in MYC's Bible college after finishing high school, with a view to serving the Lord afterwards. And all pledged that once they stood on their own feet, they would help take care of the other orphans.

"We will not forget our younger brothers and sisters!" they would assure Papa and Mama, who would always smile with satisfaction upon hearing their words.

Although the responsibilities involved in running a large-scale orphan ministry were heavy, David knew that he could not turn back from his promise to God to "do those ministries that no one else wanted to do." True, the Lord was providing much of the day-to-day orphanage expenses through ANM and another U.S. Christian organization, World Help. But even so, it was MYC who was responsible day in and day out to feed, clothe, educate, discipline and guide nearly 100 children from diverse cultural and religious backgrounds. The work was never easy. But the MYC children's ministry team looked daily to God for strength and wisdom for the task.

Aside from helping drug addicts, lepers, and orphans, there was yet another group of "outcasts" that the Lord led David to serve—HIV-AIDS patients. From the late 1980s onward, more and more of the addicts entering MYC's drug rehab program were testing positive for HIV. All of them had contracted the disease from using dirty drug needles. Most of the institutions, hospitals and treatment centers in Myanmar would have nothing to do with HIV+ patients, as they feared contamination. But David, remembering his commitment to God to do those ministries that no one else wanted to do, decided that he would boldly welcome such patients in his midst.

"You're insane!" argued many people, including Christian supporters of his ministry. "How can you mix HIV+ patients with the other residents? It's far too dangerous! You'll all die together!"

It was a daring experiment, no doubt. But David had a peace from the Lord that this was the right thing to do. As soon as MYC began admitting HIV+ addicts, David brought in medical doctors to educate the entire community about HIV-AIDS. The doctors explained how the AIDS virus was transmitted (through blood, sex, and needles) and how it was not (through mosquito bites or saliva). They described the symptoms of HIV and the onset of full-blown AIDS. They answered all kinds of questions posed by the residents and the Bible college students. The medical presentation greatly helped to calm everyone's fears and put them at ease, so much so that David decided to make this a regular part of MYC's curriculum.

"Even if everyone else—including the Christian community—treats them as outcasts, I will make sure they are treated with respect, dignity, and love at MYC!" David firmly told his staff.

As such, HIV+ residents were not kept separate from the others. Everyone studied together, ate together, worshipped together, and slept in the same dorms. A doctor friend of David who worked with the UN began supplying MYC with free HIV-AIDS medication to help stem the progress of the disease. David also supplied them with regular multi-vitamins to boost their immune systems. Many residents continued to enjoy reasonably good health while going through the program, but inevitably some would get progressively sicker and die before finishing their three-year course. Naturally, such events made the other residents even more aware of the fragility of life and the importance of living each day wisely for the Lord.

Several MYC graduates went on to break cultural taboos by talking openly about their HIV+ status in front of large crowds. M. Jala was one of these bold evangelists, a Kachin from Northern Shan State. When he enrolled in MYC's rehab program in 1991, he tested positive for HIV. The staff didn't share this news with him immediately, because they wanted him to grow stronger in his new faith before telling him. When he learned later that he had already contracted HIV, he remained calm and entrusted the rest of his days to the Lord.

After graduating from MYC in 1994, Jala stayed on as staff. He began testifying boldly at MYC crusades about how he had contracted HIV, warning others to flee from drugs to avoid this terrible disease. Many Burmese were shocked at his openness, as such things were usually covered up instead of publicized. But Jala and his fellow HIV+ evangelists were hardly concerned about preserving their self-image. Rather, they were all too willing to disclose their mistakes, if by doing so they could discourage other Burmese youth from making the same wrong choices.

Papa David bringing gifts of food and clothing to the
orphan children at Myanchaung (1996)

Children standing in front of the newly-constructed
MYC orphanage at Thanlyin (1999)

MYC orphans enjoying a meal at Thanlyin (1999)

Kevin Yone Mo with three newly-baptized HIV-AIDS patients

Over the years, MYC gradually became well-known nationally for its willingness to openly discuss the HIV-AIDS issue in public forums and also to boldly accept HIV+ residents in its program. Even the UN took note of MYC's progressive stance on this issue and approached David again. This time, they wanted help with their HIV-AIDS awareness campaigns.

"We know that even with our huge budget, we would have a hard time drawing the same crowds you do at your rallies," admitted the UN officials to David.

"I don't draw the crowds," said David frankly. "It's the Lord who brings them."

Nodding awkwardly, the UN officials continued. "We have a substantial UN budget for HIV-AIDS awareness, and we feel that MYC would make an excellent national partner in helping us get our message out. In fact, you're already doing it, and honestly speaking, you're doing it better than most other organizations."

David smiled politely but remained calm. He had been through this before, and he was waiting to see what the catch would be.

"You just need to write an implementation plan and submit it to us, explaining how MYC plans to achieve our HIV-AIDS awareness goals with UN funds. You're already touching on most of our awareness points in your presentations. The only major point that you need to add is explaining the importance of condom use if you have HIV-AIDS, because that can greatly reduce the …"

David abruptly interrupted the UN official, saying, "I'm sorry, but there's no need to go any further. Condoms and Jesus Christ don't go together! Thank you for your offer, but we'll stick to what we're doing!"

As the years went by, over half of the addicts entering MYC's rehab program started testing positive for HIV. David would never inform them right away; rather, he would typically wait at least a year before giving them the news, so they would have time to grow in spiritual maturity. When he felt the time was right, he would personally inform them of their HIV+ status, pray with them, and encourage them to look to the Lord for healing. Amazingly, several addicts who were HIV+ upon admission to MYC later tested negative after fervent prayer. Such testimonies naturally encouraged the HIV+ residents to continue walking closely with the Lord.

David began to realize that he needed to drastically expand his outreach to HIV-AIDS patients. Their numbers had mushroomed nationally, and the disease had now spread beyond the male drug addict population to include addicts' wives and also commercial sex workers. Medication for HIV-AIDS patients was extremely expensive and out of the reach of most patients. Moreover, there were pitifully few places in the country where patients could actually go and receive proper medical treatment. Most of the country's hospitals immediately turned them away once they discovered they had HIV-AIDS.

Keeping all these things in mind, David felt that it was high time that Myanmar's Christians take the lead in reaching out to those suffering from this disease. As a result, in 2002 MYC became the first non-profit organization in the country to open an HIV-AIDS hospice. David had the 16-bed center constructed right within the Hmawbi campus, so that patients would be able to join the Bible college and rehab center routines and not feel isolated. Many of the initial patients were MYC graduates and MYC staff, whose AIDS symptoms had suddenly taken a turn for the worse. David also accepted female patients, including girls who had contracted the disease through marriage to HIV+ men. He arranged for free medicines from the UN as well as regular visits from a Christian doctor. Many patients openly testified that their own natural families had not shown them even a fraction of the love and concern that David had.

Drug addicts, orphans, lepers, and HIV-AIDS patients—all of these outcast groups found Christian refuge and love in David's heart and ministry. Many outsiders considered David crazy for taking them all in, and at times he also wondered if he had gone too far. But every time he started to question his sanity, he would remember the words of Jesus

Christ: *Whatever you did for one of the least of these brothers of mine, you did it for me.* (Matthew 25:40) And with renewed inspiration he would pray, *Lord, it's not easy at all doing this, but I promised that I would do those ministries that no one else wanted to do. Just give me extra grace, and I'll keep doing it!*

The Lord indeed gave David plenty of extra grace, for He found in David a willing heart. And through his example of selfless and sacrificial love, countless believers in Myanmar and around the world were challenged to a higher level of spiritual commitment for Jesus Christ.

CHAPTER 16
Not of This World
(1995-2002)

"**W**e're number one! Can you believe it? We're number one!" shouted David jubilantly to his staff. "Praise the Lord! Hallelujah!"

There it was, printed for the whole world to see. MYC's newly-released album, *Not of This World* (1998), hit the number one spot on the nation's Top 10 secular album charts. It was the first time that a Christian album had risen to the top of the secular rankings, and David knew that this was nothing less than a miracle from God.

Although MYC's focus always remained on ministering to the social outcasts of Myanmar, the organization over time became best known nationally for its music. This was natural: the MYC Praise Band and its secular counterpart, Iron Cross, was comprised of the nation's top musicians. This in turn enabled them to attract the country's best vocalists to record and sing along with them. The result? Across the country, young people from both Buddhist and Christian backgrounds alike found their music to be as good as, if not better than, that of the other pop bands.

Everyone knew that rock-and-roll guitarist Saw Bwe Hmu was God's gift to MYC, as it was he who launched MYC's gospel music ministry onto the national scene. Of course, Saw also felt that MYC was God's gift to him, because the ten years he spent there were the happiest years of his life. In fact, he was so happy at MYC that he put on a great deal of weight and eventually weighed over 300 pounds. Not surprisingly, he suffered a massive heart attack in 1995 and suddenly passed away. The entire MYC family mourned his death as a great loss for God's kingdom.

Fortunately, Saw Bwe Hmu's musical genius did not pass away with his death. At David's request several years earlier, Saw had begun raising up a musical disciple to succeed him: the young Chit San Maung. Chit had been attending Sunday School and church at MYC since he was 15 years old, after his family moved to Yangon. The teenager possessed an unusual gift for music: at the age of five he was already playing the guitar, and by age 15 he was leading his own band. David quickly spotted Chit's talent and encouraged Saw to mentor him.

Saw Bwe Hmu willingly taught the young man everything he knew, and in a short while it became evident to all that Chit would one day surpass his mentor. David began to involve him in various MYC outreach programs, and Chit quickly developed his own unique style of guitar playing. David liked what he saw in him: his musical giftedness, his eagerness to learn, and his desire to serve the Lord. So when Chit later asked David for permission to marry his daughter, Sharon, he gladly agreed! Shortly after their marriage in 1995, the same year that Saw passed away, Chit joined MYC as a full-time musician.

After Saw's death, it was up to Chit to take MYC's music ministry forward. He had big shoes to fill: without Saw Bwe Hmu as the main draw, would the crowds still be interested in listening to MYC's gospel message? But the Lord was with Chit and enabled him to quickly win the hearts of the masses, just as Saw had done a generation earlier.

In particular, God blessed Chit with the rare ability to master various guitar tricks, which he began performing on a regular basis wherever he played. He would play the guitar with his feet. He would pluck melodies on guitar strings with his teeth and with his tongue. He would put the guitar behind his head and play. He would set the guitar down upright on its stand and play it with two hands, like a piano. The crowds were thrilled with his antics, and they kept on coming to MYC events to see more of him. Before long, Chit was dubbed as "the new

#1 guitarist in Myanmar," having successfully stepped into the shoes of his late mentor, Saw Bwe Hmu.

Even though David praised God for the addition of Chit San Maung to MYC's music team, he knew that having a great guitarist on board wasn't the only key to a successful music ministry. Equally important was having a gifted songwriter who could capture universal Christian truths, express them in heartfelt lyrics, and set them to soul-stirring music. Of course, different people had written songs for MYC over the years, and some of them had turned out fairly well. But now that God had brought world-class musicians to MYC, it seemed only fitting that there should be a world-class songwriter to supply them with music.

Lord, you know what we need, prayed David. *You gave us Saw Bwe Hmu, and now you've given us Chit San Maung. Could you also give us a good songwriter, so we could bring you even more glory?*

The Lord wonderfully answered David's prayer in the person of Saw Lwin Lwin. A Karen from Northern Shan State, Saw began using alcohol and drugs during his teenage years and eventually became hooked on heroin. A gifted singer-songwriter, he made his way to Yangon in 1990 at the age of 30 and got a job with the music department of a mainline Christian denomination. By day he would compose and sing gospel songs, and by night he would secretly sing in nightclubs. He quit heroin once he was hired, but he continued to drink and use other chemical substances.

Some of his fellow singers grew increasingly concerned about Saw's drug use and brought him to MYC in 1996. But the tattooed man with the waist-length hair was too proud to admit that he had a problem. Even so, Papa David and Mama Kathy welcomed him in their midst and told him that they would always be willing to help him, whenever he was ready.

Saw's life continued to go downhill, and he became more and more disillusioned with life. One day while visiting MYC in 1998, he found himself looking deep into Papa's and Mama's eyes. In their gaze he saw God's great love and mercy, and suddenly he was overwhelmed with sorrow over his own sin. He felt as if the Lord was asking him to surrender everything to Him. That very day he threw away his cigarettes and drugs and prayed to receive Jesus Christ as his Savior. At last he had experienced the love of God!

After he was born-again, Saw was filled with a desire to genuinely serve the Lord. He realized regretfully that over the past many years, all the gospel songs he had written had come from his head, not from his heart. He had spent countless hours reading the Bible and listening to sermons for "inspiration" for his gospel songs, while all that time he was spiritually dead. Now that he had truly come to know the love of God, he could not wait to compose real gospel songs from his heart. David quickly recognized God's transforming work in him and brought him on board as MYC staff.

The first album that Saw Lwin Lwin composed—*Not of This World* (1998)—made it to the number one spot on the Top 10 list in the secular album rankings. He gave all the glory to God for this achievement: the songs were simply an expression of the joy and gratitude he felt in his heart for what the Lord had done in his life. So many fans kept on calling the MYC office to ask about the meaning of the songs that David had to appoint someone to sit by the phone all day just to answer questions and share the gospel. The album's most popular song, "The Greatness," recounted his own story of how God had birthed new life in him through Jesus.

The Greatness

The beautiful creation of the universe
The handiwork of God in the heavens
The power of the clouds and thunder
Witness to eternity.
The voices of birds and beautiful scenery
Full of praises and singing
Playing with the breeze in motion
Gush forth with living water.

Chorus:

Oh my soul, praise the Lord
For the greatness of God.
Oh my soul, again give praise
For the greatness of God.

For God so loved the world
He gave his life because He loved us.
He paid for our punishment on the cross
For the remission of sins by His blood.
When he comes in his glory
There will be joy and peace.
Praise the Lord, hallelujah!

For David, Saw and Chit, their greatest joy was to see the gospel message reaching thousands of Burmese hearts through the album sales. People who had never set foot in a church were hearing about the love of Christ every time they listened to the album songs. "Where we cannot go, our music can go!" proclaimed David excitedly. For indeed, this was the original intention behind David's first MYC album adventure many years ago: to preach the gospel through music.

The huge profits from the album were an additional blessing for the ministry. MYC was able to purchase top-quality musical instruments and speakers from overseas, as well as set aside enough money to finance future albums.

Under the guidance of the Holy Spirit, Saw Lwin Lwin continued to churn out new songs for the Lord and for MYC. Sometimes he would disappear for three or four days at a time to pray, read the Bible, and compose songs. Common themes in his lyrics included the return of Christ, the Christian life, drug addicts, orphans, lepers and HIV-AIDS patients. He would masterfully set these themes and lyrics to a blend of country jazz, pop rock, and heavy metal music styles. The result was cutting-edge music that appealed to a broad cross-section of Myanmar's listening audience, both Christian and non-Christian.

For example, one popular song titled "Hero of the Gospel" (from MYC's 2000 album, *In the House of God*) brilliantly captured in words and music the heroic sacrifices made by Christian evangelists:

Hero of the Gospel

Those who sow in tears
Will reap with songs of joy
Bravely he sets out for the gospel
Unknown to others as he goes out to a jungle tribe
In the midst of mountains and valleys
Goes the evangelist whom we love
Pressing on with great sacrifice
Giving thanks and praise despite his fatigue
Day and night he goes on preaching
The good news of Jesus Christ.

Chorus:
Hero, hero, for the kingdom of God
Hero, hero, willing to give his life
For the kingdom of God.

From his bosom comes out holy love
For men who don't know Christ and are living in darkness
He sleeps with snakes and scorpions in thorn-filled jungles
He crosses cold rivers to take the gospel
Even if his bones have to tremble
His clothes are wet from dew and rain
He keeps going on foot in spite of blood and sweat
To share a gift with a faraway people
It pleases him to minister with suffering
As his forefathers and other holy brothers have done
In the midst of the thick forest he lays down his life
Unknown to any other
Up to the house of God he goes.

Over the years, MYC produced more than 20 albums, which were distributed all over the country and also to Burmese communities overseas. David made it a point to sing on every album, which gave a sense of continuity and tradition to the MYC series. And with Saw Lwin Lwin writing the songs and Chit San Maung on lead guitar, the MYC Praise Band and its secular counterpart Iron Cross quickly emerged as Myanmar's leading rock band.

Wherever the band went, they always drew huge crowds. Typically they would play a mix of country jazz, Asian pop, and heavy metal, to appeal to both younger and older listeners. Fans simply couldn't get enough of their music and of Chit's guitar tricks. In appearance, they looked like a typical Western heavy-metal rock band: long black hair, black T-shirts and dark jeans. But despite their rough look, their message was always the same: Jesus, Jesus, Jesus!

When they were not on tour, the MYC Praise Band would play every Sunday afternoon at the MYC headquarters church in Yangon. There were actually two services held on Sundays: a traditional service in the morning for the older crowd, and a youth service in the afternoon featuring contemporary music. Typically 600 to 700 Burmese youth would attend the afternoon service, making it arguably the most popular youth service in the country. The fellowship hall would consistently be packed to capacity by 2:30 p.m., even though the service would start only at 4:00 p.m. (Latecomers would have to sit in the overflow area and watch the service via TV monitor.)

Naturally, the main draw of the service was the music, and both believers and non-believers alike flocked there week after week to hear their favorite band. Many in the crowd would have already memorized the songs, and each week a few individuals would be given the special opportunity to sing on stage with the band. Of course, David always made sure that the excellent music was followed by an even better sermon. Through this outreach, countless young people heard the gospel clearly preached, and many of them surrendered their lives to Jesus Christ.

With the soaring nationwide popularity of MYC's music came even greater opportunities to share the gospel through crusades. David's goal was to reach every state of Myanmar with the message God had entrusted to him, and he realized this would be possible using the band as a draw. He began targeting new areas of the country in which to conduct crusades, enlisting the help of local churches whenever possible. Once the dates and venues were settled, he would then contact several nationally-known vocalists in advance and request them to donate their singing talent for the crusade. Most would happily agree, knowing that MYC had an excellent track record for dealing with drug abuse and HIV-AIDS.

The presence of top vocalists along with the MYC Praise Band ensured that MYC's three-day crusades would be attended by huge crowds—often 50,000 to 100,000 in rural places. As usual, the crusades would feature a lively mix of music, testimonies, social awareness messages (drug abuse and HIV-AIDS prevention), and gospel preaching. By the end of each crusade, thousands—and sometimes even tens of thousands—would stand up to accept Jesus Christ as the first step to a new, transformed life.

"Remember," David would remind his staff, "that we can't take any credit for this ourselves. We're all a bunch of drug addicts, alcoholics, and sinners, whom God is choosing to use. All the glory goes to Jesus alone!"

It was true. The phenomenal success of MYC's music ministry was definitely not of this world. David knew it, and he made sure his staff knew it. As a result, God chose to continue working miracle after miracle through this diverse group of lions-turned-lambs.

A sampling of MYC album covers,
featuring innovative designs
appealing to the nation's youth

David recording an album song in the MYC studio (1996)

An MYC gospel crusade in the Naga and Chin regions of western Myanmar (2000)

A typical MYC gospel crusade crowd of many thousands, bundled up and sitting on the ground at night (2002)

A typical MYC gospel crusade featuring the nation's top vocalists and instrumentalists. Chit San Maung is playing at right. (1997)

Chit San Maung performing his trademark guitar tricks at
an MYC gospel crusade (1997)

David addressing the crowd at the close of an MYC gospel crusade (1998)

CHAPTER 17
Never Say Die
(1997-2003)

"Papa," sobbed David's daughter Sharon over the phone, "Mama has cancer! The doctor said it doesn't look good at all. Oh Papa, please come back home quickly! Mama needs you!"

David was stunned. A few weeks earlier, Kathy had complained of a stomach ache, so David had taken her for a medical checkup. The doctor assured them that it was nothing serious and prescribed her some pills for pain relief. David grew concerned because Kathy had started to pass blood, but she told him that it would probably clear up shortly as the doctor had said.

Thinking that all was well, David left with MYC's crusade team and traveled north to Kalemyo, Sagaing Division, where a series of crusade meetings were scheduled for March 1997. The crusades went exceptionally well, and thousands had come forward to accept the Lord. He was in high spirits and looking forward to returning home, when all of a sudden he received Sharon's phone call.

Kathy had been diagnosed with advanced uterine cancer. The disease had already spread throughout her body, which was the reason for her bleeding. The doctor gave her a 50% chance of survival.

"I'm coming back as soon as I can," answered David. His normally confident voice had suddenly become shaky. "Be sure to take good care of Mama until I get there."

Lord, this can't be! cried David. How would he survive without her? For 34 years she had stood beside him every step of the way, serving as a mother not only to his five natural children but also to all the drug addicts and orphans. Kathy was the backbone of his ministry and his family. *God, how can you take her away?*

As he rushed back to Yangon, he suddenly regretted that all these years he had never taken Kathy along with him on any of his trips. She had always wanted to accompany him, but the huge responsibilities of child-rearing and cooking for the entire MYC community had kept her at home. She used to always tell David before he set out, "Don't worry about me, and don't worry about us here—I'll take care of everything at home!" Even when he was away ministering for weeks at a stretch, she would never complain but would always be supportive.

Lord, what will I do without Kathy? pleaded David prayerfully. *Please don't take her away from me right now!*

With thousands of Christians across Myanmar and America praying for her healing, Kathy underwent intense radiation and radium treatment in Yangon. In spite of all her pain and suffering, she kept on encouraging David to look up to the Lord. "Stay calm, don't worry about me, and leave everything in God's hands," Kathy kept on reminding her husband. "Remember, all eyes in the ministry are focused on your reaction to this situation!"

After two months of cancer treatment, David began to sense in his spirit that the Lord had healed Kathy. Her condition improved greatly and her strength returned. David wanted to take her to Singapore to have a thorough medical exam to see if the cancer had really left her body. As she did not have a passport, he promptly applied for one.

Several months passed, but still Kathy's passport did not arrive. Upon further inquiry, David discovered the reason for the delay. Previously the government had requested him to represent Myanmar at the Fourth World Congress on HIV-AIDS in Manila, Philippines, but he had declined their invitation. He now understood that Kathy's passport would not be issued unless he complied with their request. Believing that God had a special plan in all this, he informed them that he had changed his mind and would now be able to attend. Kathy's passport was issued shortly thereafter.

Never in their married life had Kathy ever accompanied David on any of his trips. So it was a special gift from God that both of them could finally travel together—and that too, overseas. They left in October 1997 and their first stop was Manila. While David attended the HIV-AIDS Congress, Kathy was able to visit her family in the Philippines, whom she had not seen in over 20 years. How they both praised God for working things out so beautifully!

From Manila they then traveled to Singapore, where David through his network of friends arranged for Kathy to be examined by a good doctor. To their amazement, the doctor announced that all the cancer cells had dried up in her body! David and Kathy were thrilled beyond words and kept on praising God for answering the prayers of so many.

Interestingly, MYC's ministry exploded with growth during the period of Kathy's illness. David shared that the spiritual fruit in 1997 was roughly equivalent to that of the previous five years put together. An unprecedented number of people, many of them Buddhists, had accepted the Lord through MYC's ministry. As a result, many new home fellowships were started and many new church buildings were constructed. Moreover, different government agencies and even several UN organizations had approached MYC for assistance in combating drug abuse. David wondered if Satan had attacked Kathy precisely because he knew that God was working so mightily through MYC.

Kathy's condition continued to improve after returning home to Yangon. As an expression of thanksgiving to the Lord, she cooked a special Christmas dinner for 150 people. For the entire MYC community, this was the greatest Christmas gift that God could have given them that year.

From that time on, David began taking Kathy along with him on his ministry tours. That December, David and his team of 35 MYC preachers, vocalists and musicians conducted crusades in five different

David and Kathy in Singapore for Kathy's cancer treatment (1997)

Kathy preparing the Christmas Day feast in Yangon after her recovery (1997)

cities. All together, nearly half a million people heard the gospel, and many of them came forward to receive Jesus Christ into their lives. As a result of this, MYC was able to plant several new churches in these locations. In March 1998 MYC organized another series of large-scale crusades on the Myanmar-Thailand border in Kentung and Tachilek, known as the "Sodom and Gomorrah of the Golden Triangle." Over 400,000 people came out to hear the excellent music and preaching, and thousands of drug addicts, commercial sex workers and HIV-AIDS victims surrendered their lives to Jesus Christ.

Kathy was amazed by everything she saw. She kept on telling David, "I never really realized how much work for the Lord you were doing! How could you accomplish so much in such a short period of time? You really have done so much for the Lord! After seeing all this, I can now die in peace!"

After enjoying good health for a few months, Kathy again started to experience pain in her abdomen. David took her back to Singapore in June 1998 for a medical exam, where to their great dismay they learned that she had a large tumor pressing against her kidney. Immediately

The MYC team traveling to the Myanmar-Thailand border in the Golden Triangle to conduct a gospel crusade. Left of David are Albert Howard and Peter Bo; right of him are Peter Ling and Kathy. (1998)

the doctors began chemotherapy treatments, followed by surgical removal of her bladder and colon. After nearly four months of medical treatment, the doctors informed David that they had done all they could possibly do, and that now he should take her home and let her peacefully enjoy the rest of her days among family and friends.

When they arrived back in Yangon in October 1998, David was swamped with work due to the overwhelming growth of the ministry. With the help of ANM donors, MYC completed five new church buildings, constructed a permanent orphanage at Thanlyin, and extended its main fellowship hall (which was bursting at the seams due to the huge crowds attending Sunday services). Fifty of the 150 Bible school students graduated, and David brought on many of them as new ministry staff. MYC rented the National Theater in downtown Yangon for a December youth rally. The place was filled to capacity and the rally was broadcast on national television, giving huge glory to the name of Jesus. Buoyed by this huge success, MYC scheduled ten more gospel rallies to be held that same month.

But even as the ministry kept on progressing, Kathy's health steadily declined. This time, David knew that she would not be at his side much longer. As a result, he temporarily handed over many of his responsibilities to Peter Bo and Peter Ling so he could spend more time with her.

On April 24, 1999, Kathy asked David to sit at her bedside the whole day. She was in a great deal of pain, and David could hardly bear to see her suffering so much. Even so, she told him, "You must be strong in your faith until the end!" To take her mind off her pain, David showed her videotapes of the recent MYC rallies and of the messages he had recently preached.

But by late afternoon, it was clear that Kathy's strength was quickly ebbing away. She called out to David in a quiet voice, and he took her hand. Looking into his eyes, she faintly whispered, "I'm going." Then she quietly slipped away into the eternal presence of the Lord. She was 57 years old.

David with daughter Sharon at Kathy's funeral service (1999)

Kathy was buried next to David's mother, Elizabeth, in Sawbwagyi Cemetery, Yangon. She had asked David to preach the gospel at her funeral, but on that day he was not sure if he would be able to. Thousands of people from all walks of life had come to pay their last respects to Kathy, including both church and military leaders. The stage and the cemetery were blanketed with several trucks' worth of flowers.

David at Kathy's tomb (1999)

Greatly moved upon seeing this huge outpouring of love for his wife, David decided he needed to preach. But what brought tears to everyone's eyes was when the orphan children came up and sang a song for their beloved Mama. Among all, it was Kathy's orphans who cried the most that day: they knew that no one would ever replace her in their lives.

David took time to grieve, yet he knew that he had to keep on pressing forward for the Lord. He knew that immersing himself in God's work would help take his mind off of his painful loss. The new orphanage at Thanlyin was now in full swing; and every time David visited, he would think how delighted Kathy would have been to see the children thoroughly enjoying their new home. In July 1999 he dedicated the newly-constructed Hmawbi campus, home to MYC's new drug rehab center and Bible college. He continued to conduct gospel meetings and crusades all over the country, especially in the border regions. God continued to bless these outreaches, enabling MYC to plant an average of two new churches every month—making it the country's fastest-growing church-planting ministry.

The pain of Kathy's loss was cushioned by the fact that David was still surrounded by many loving family members. Twenty-eight people continued to live with him: his daughter Sharon, her husband Chit San Maung and their three children; his son David and his wife Gina; his son Timothy; and 20 orphan children ages 4 to 14! Sharon took over Kathy's job of cooking for the entire MYC community, as well as looking after the orphans. Sons David and Timothy worked as sound engineers in MYC's recording studio. Son Kevin lived nearby with his wife and two children and headed up MYC's drug rehabilitation program at the Hmawbi campus. The comfort of having his own adult children serving next to him in the ministry, as well as having his five precious grandchildren nearby, kept David active and content.

David continued to spend his days fully engaged in the Lord's work. Every morning he would be up by 5:30 a.m. and in his office by 7:00 a.m. After praying with his staff, counseling drug addicts, and attending to various church and office matters, he would drive either 30 miles north to the Hmawbi drug rehab center or 18 miles south to the Thanlyin orphanage. There he would eat lunch and spend the day visiting, counseling, and building relationships. On some days when he visited Hmawbi, he would continue on 20 miles north to visit the Myanchaung leper colony. Usually he would return back to Yangon by 5:00 p.m., exercise for an hour, and spend the rest of the evening relaxing with family.

Visiting the orphanage was always a special source of joy for him, as the nearly 100 children would rush to Papa to recite their newly-memorized Bible verses or sing songs for him. David would always tell the staff, "If you're getting fat and the children are getting thin, then there's a problem. But if the children are getting fat and you're getting thin, then that's good!"

He would also repeatedly ask the children, "Do you love this place?" When they all would answer in the affirmative, he would reply back, "Then one day when you grow up and become leaders, you must look after your friends and the other children who will be staying here!"

"We will!" they would all answer happily.

"But you can do this only if you have the love of Jesus in your hearts," David would lovingly warn.

With huge smiles they would shout back, "We do!"

In the summer of 2001, David visited the United States to accept an honorary doctorate degree in humanities from Liberty University (Lynchburg, Virginia). Over the years as Liberty University had partnered with MYC in providing many of their books as well as their Bible correspondence course, its leadership had come to appreciate David's extraordinary achievements for the kingdom of God. David gave all the glory to the Lord for this huge honor. The degree would definitely give the ministry of MYC extra credibility and stature.

In the early part of 2002, David began experiencing a strange pain in his abdomen. Even after visiting the doctor several times and taking different medicines, the pain did not go away. He then began to suspect that he had cancer. His suspicions were confirmed after he got the results of a biopsy.

Initially, the news shattered David's calm, and his immediate reaction was fear. But then he thought to himself, *Why should I be frightened? I've been preaching to others about life after death, so why should I myself be frightened? After all, isn't the motto of my ministry, "Never Say Die"?*

Remembering Kathy's final words to him—"you must be strong until the end"—David resolved to live life and fight death with the same determination that had characterized the rest of his life. As he frankly shared the news of his cancer with different groups of people—addicts, Bible students, orphans and lepers—their reaction was always the same: tears of devastation.

"Can't we give our lives in your place?" the lepers wailed. They considered it a cruel twist of fate that he, rather than they, should be facing death.

"No," David would always answer with a smile. "We all have our own time, as determined by God. But remember: never say die!"

After entrusting the different facets of MYC's ministry to his senior leaders, David left for Singapore in April 2002 to undergo medical treatment for terminal liver cancer. The doctors gave him a 50% chance of surviving beyond five months. Even so, David was determined to fight it out as best as he could, as he truly believed there were a few more things he had left to do before going to his eternal home.

Accordingly, the doctors immediately started him on multiple, aggressive rounds of radiation and chemotherapy treatments, which greatly sapped his energy. As a result, the illness brought David to his deepest low ever. Never in his life had he experienced such discouragement—not even when he was dying from hepatitis 28 years ago. Back then, he had nothing to live for; now he had so much to live for. The man who was literally called "Papa" by thousands and who had spent the last 28 years encouraging hundreds of thousands now desperately needed encouragement himself. But God was faithful in supplying this need through the emails and prayers of thousands of well-wishers in Myanmar and the U.S.

Even while he was undergoing treatment in Singapore, David continued to handle much of MYC's office work from his laptop and maintained regular contact with his staff through email and phone. Although he knew that his staff sorely felt his prolonged absence, he also realized that they were learning to depend fully upon the Lord and not on him. This was extremely important, as the reins of leadership would have to be handed over to them in the near future.

In mid-August, David requested and received a two-week leave from his doctors to return home to make arrangements for an upcoming pastors' conference in October. During his brief visit to Yangon, the Lord gave him strength to preach seven times. Whenever he spoke, his message was the same: "Remember, your inheritance is Jesus! You don't have anything else in the world except Jesus. If you have Jesus, you have everything! If you don't have Jesus, you have nothing! Everything you see in this life—it's just fleeting. Soon we'll all be seeing the new heaven and the new earth. Remember the promise of eternal life: never say die!"

During the same visit, David was also able to attend the dedication of MYC's HIV Hospice Center, a project he had dreamed about for many years and had worked hard to bring to reality. Approximately a thousand people attended the occasion, and he thanked the Lord for enabling him to see another one of his dreams for the kingdom of God coming true.

After returning to Singapore for further treatment, David requested and received another short leave to go to Yangon in October to attend two important events. One was the commencement exercises of MYC's Bible College, in which 96 students graduated. The other was the large pastors' conference, which was attended by nearly 200 pastors and evangelists from different tribes and ethnic groups all over Myanmar. Once again, David praised the Lord for greatly refreshing his spirit and giving him new resolve to continue serving Him.

To the surprise of his Singaporean doctors, David requested a third leave from his cancer treatments to visit home, this time for three weeks in late December-early January. In spite of his sickness, he was determined to participate in at least one more MYC crusade. His staff had already made preparations for the December crusade to be held in a remote region, which would involve difficult travel via elephants. Naturally they had their doubts as to whether David should go along, given the state of his health. But David was determined to join the elephant safari through the jungles and up to the mountains, in order to preach the gospel to the lost. He knew that this crusade might be his last, and he wanted to finish his race well.

David atop an elephant on his way to an MYC gospel crusade.
By now he had already contracted cancer. (2002)

The Lord gave great grace to David, helping him to withstand the rough elephant journey through the malaria-infested Tharrawaddy jungle. Nearly 50,000 came out to attend the crusade. After David had

David in Singapore for cancer treatment (2002)

finished his message and given the invitation, about 60% of those present decided to accept Jesus Christ! Again, he gave all the glory to God. The doctors had not expected him to live this long, yet here he was—in the middle of a remote jungle wilderness—leading thousands of new believers to the feet of Jesus.

David returned to Singapore in January 2003 for another round of treatments. But in early March, he prayerfully made the decision to return back to Myanmar and resume the work the Lord had placed on his heart. He had undergone nearly a year's worth of cancer treatments in Singapore, and his condition had stabilized. He sorely missed having his large family around him and the constant interaction with addicts, orphans, lepers and Bible students. If his health was not going to significantly improve any more in Singapore, then he wanted to spend the rest of his days living and serving among his own people.

Shortly after reaching Myanmar in March, David had to undergo emergency surgery to remove a huge tumor wrapped around his spine. There he continued his chemotherapy treatments at a local hospital, under the care of a Christian doctor. In spite of his physical weakness, David continued to participate in as many MYC activities as his health would allow. In the meantime, he was satisfied to see MYC's day-to-day operations being handled efficiently by the new leadership team he had appointed in his absence.

However in May, David's health took another serious downturn, and his family forced him to go back to Singapore for further treatment. For three months he continued to be subjected to a battery of medical tests and procedures, and the doctors again gave him a 50-50 chance of survival. But David had long ago stopped being bothered by such odds. He knew that his life was in God's hands, and he was confident that the Lord would not take him away until his work was finished.

In August, David again requested a two-week medical leave to return home to make arrangements for the annual MYC pastors' conference in October. He left Singapore for Yangon on August 13 and planned to return back on August 30.

But David never made it back to Singapore. Within days after returning home, his condition quickly deteriorated and he was immediately hospitalized. On the morning of August 24, he vomited a great deal of blood and lapsed into a semi-coma, from which he never recovered. That very night, in the presence of his loved ones, he slipped away into eternal glory. He was 59 years old.

As the news of David's death made its way to the people of Yangon and beyond, tens of thousands mourned the passing of a true Christian hero. In the meantime, his family quietly made preparations for his funeral service, remembering what he had instructed them prior to his death. He wanted to be buried with his hands clasped together on his chest, with his index fingers pointing up towards heaven. It had always been his trademark gesture, and he wanted to be remembered by it.

At his funeral service held three days later, an uncountable sea of people gathered to pay their last respects to David: family, friends, drug addicts, alcoholics, lepers, orphans, Bible students, pastors, musicians, church members, military leaders and ordinary Yangon citizens. Many silently wept under the clear blue sky as they heard the eulogy.

But somewhere else that day, in a land far above that same blue sky, one man was feeling healthier and happier than he had ever felt before. He had truly fought the good fight. He had indeed finished the race. And without any doubt, he had kept the faith. He had labored to be faithful to his Master until the very end, just to be able to hear the words, "Well done, good and faithful servant!" at the end of his journey.

And on that day, while the crowds below were grieving, he was rejoicing—for he had already entered into the joy of his Lord.

EPILOGUE

The ministry of Myanmar Young Crusaders has continued to advance forward after David's death, under the guidance of Jesus Christ and the able leadership team which David had diligently labored to raise up.

Drug addicts continue to be delivered; orphans, lepers and HIV-AIDS patients continue to receive loving Christian care; the gospel continues to be boldly preached across the nation through crusades; and new churches continue to be planted and led by MYC Bible college graduates.

For more information about the ministry of MYC and/or to learn more about how to partner with them through prayer or financial giving, please contact:

ANM
P.O. Box 5303
Charlottesville, VA 22905

Phone: 540-456-7111
Email: anm@adnamis.org

NEVER SAY DIE!

LaVergne, TN USA
16 October 2009
161131LV00001BC/1/P